how does Jesus help me stop worrying?

What should I do in scarry storms?

how do I know Jesus loves me?

To

h.e.e.

From

Jell Breeecoe

Date

JESUS

Makes a Major Comeback
And Other Amazing Feats

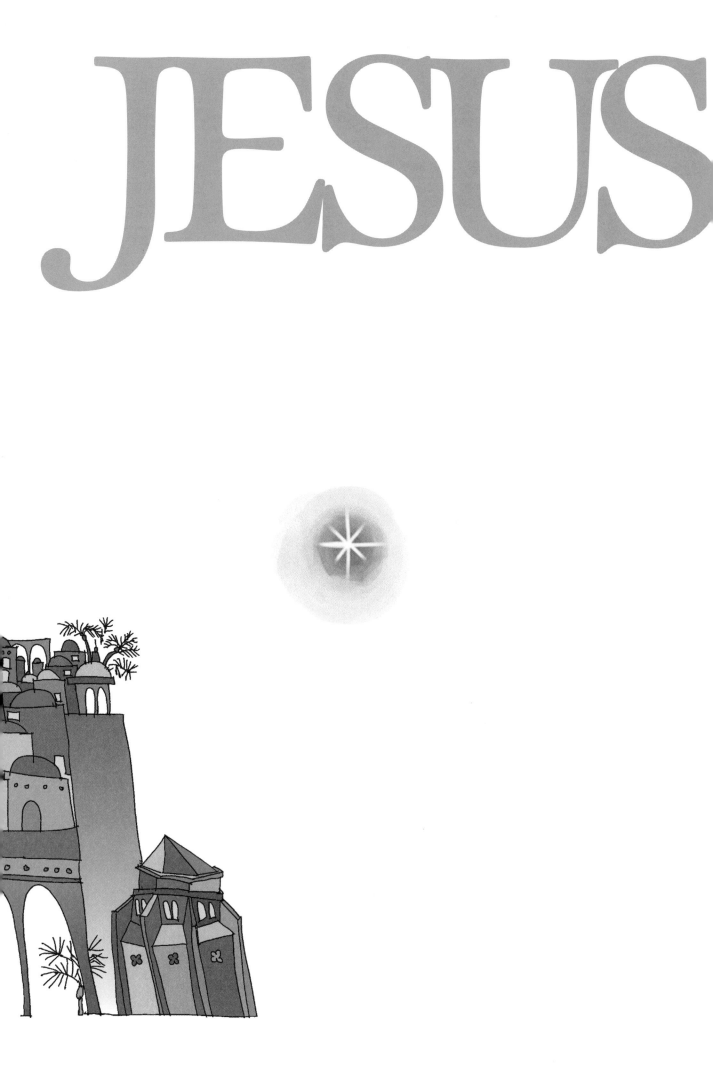

Makes a Major Comeback

And Other Amazing Feats

JILL & STUART BRISCOE
pictures and cartoons by **RUSS FLINT**
music by **LARRY MOORE**

 Baker Books

A Division of Baker Book House Co
Grand Rapids, Michigan 49516

Text copyright 1996 by Jill and Stuart Briscoe
Music copyright 1996 by Larry Moore
Art copyright 1996 by Russ Flint

Published by Baker Books
a division of Baker Book House Company
P.O. Box 6287, Grand Rapids, MI 49516-6287

Printed in the United States of America

Library of Congress Cataloging-in-Publication Data

Briscoe, Jill.
    Jesus makes a major comeback: and other amazing
feats : book 3 / Jill and Stuart Briscoe : Russ Flint, illus-
trator.
        p. cm.
    ISBN 0-8010-4197-X
    1. Bible stories, English—N.T.   I. Briscoe, D. Stuart.
II. Flint, Russ.   III. Title.
BS551.2.B74 1996
221.9′505—dc20   94-36790

Unless otherwise indicated, Scripture quotations are from
the Holy Bible, New International Version®. NIV®.
Copyright 1973, 1978, 1984 by Zondervan Publishing House.
All rights reserved. Other versions used are The Living
Bible.

An accompanying tape (ISBN 0–8010-3017-X) is available
from the publisher. It features a children's group singing all
the songs in the four books and the Briscoes reading selec-
tions from the "Let's Pretend" and "Let's Make a Video" sec-
tions.

This book is produced in cooperation with Alive
Communications, Inc., 1465 Kelly Johnson Blvd., Suite 320,
Colorado Springs, CO 80920.

CONTENTS

We gratefully appreciate the following people who made this project a delight:

Betty De Vries, a wise and skillful editor, whose vision for a children's book coincided with ours and whose skill far exceeded our abilities

Kappie Griesell, who so diligently dug out the Neat Facts

Larry Moore, who took our words and added his delightful music that sets our feet tapping and our hearts singing

Russ Flint, whose art is so entrancing and interesting that we wonder if anyone will read our text

To
our grandchildren
whom we love so dearly

May this book
bring delight to your hearts
and more love
and appreciation
for the God whom we serve.

There's something special about this book

 To

catch by surprise
and to surprise with joy
freshen
and excite new attention
in the old, old story

 To

peek around the corner of a verse
and delight to see
who is coming

To

smell the smells
admire the rich clothes
and glimpse the colors
of worlds different from ours

To

break the bread of life
into small enough pieces
for young minds
to thoroughly digest

To

tell of Jesus—
from Genesis to Revelation

To

discover truths old and new
young and old
child and adult
together

To

experience
with laughter and tears
simple retelling of old stories
allowing imagination
to refresh favorite events
using songs and simple dramas
to promote understanding

To

know God better
love God more

To

share these discoveries
with a lost, hurting world
of children
and adults

To

this end
authors
artist
composer
publisher

invite you to enjoy
Book 3, *Jesus Makes Major
Comeback: And Other
Amazing Feats*!

Letter to Parents

Now that our three children are in their "thirty somethings," we realize we have been parents an aggregate of over a hundred years.

There's more!

As our children have produced nine grandchildren, at last count, we have accumulated almost forty years of grandparenting.

So you could say we have a vested interest in children.

We enjoy telling stories to youngsters, answering their questions, hearing them laugh, and watching their eyes light up with understanding. There's nothing quite like a fire, a cozy chair, a child, an adult, and a good children's book.

"Read us a story, Papa Stu," elicits a special response, especially when I have a good story available.

"Tell us about Daniel and the lions, Grandma," will energize even a fatigued senior citizen.

With these things in mind, we started to work on this project. We wanted to produce something that would convey the old, old story in a new and fresh way. Our intention was that children, long familiar with Bible stories, would be drawn to them once again because they were presented differently. How differently? Well, we are firm believers in children having their own imaginative capabilities and their special brand of humor. So "straight stories" are immediately followed by imaginative, humorous "Let's Pretend" tales.

Parents may be surprised to learn that Jonah's whale was called Wally and that the seagulls observing his watery excursion were called Beagull and Deegull, and that mountains talk to giraffes, but children will take it in their stride. And they'll love Russ Flint's pictures and cartoons and funny little sketches. They'll laugh and so will you.

Our primary aim is to lead young children and adults alike to a wider knowledge of the Book of Books. May you find these books interesting, endearing, entertaining, educational, and inspiring.

Happy reading,

Jill and Stuart

The Bible is divided into two parts called the Old Testament and the New Testament. In this book we will look at the beginning of the second part—the New Testament.

The first four books in the New Testament are called the Gospels. *Gospel* is another word for good news. We all like to hear good news, like "Aunt Judy has a new baby," or "Cousin Cameron has a new puppy." But the good news of the Gospels is the best news ever heard. The Gospels tell us that God the Son left heaven where he always lived and came to earth to live with people for a short time. The reason he came was to show how much he loves us. He came to earth as a baby named Jesus.

The Gospels tell the story of how Jesus was born, where he lived, and the wonderful things he did, including his miracles. They also tell about the people he met. Some people were nice and others were very nasty to him. Jesus healed many people who were sick and unhappy. He told the people stories that helped them to understand about God, stories we call parables. Always Jesus told the people that God wanted them to love him and each other because he loved them.

Jesus had many followers and twelve special friends called disciples or apostles. The Gospels tell many stories about the things that Jesus and his friends did together. After a short time the people who hated Jesus had him killed on a cross. But the most wonderful thing

THE GOSP

happened—he came back from the dead! The disciples could not believe it was true. But Jesus showed them it was true. This was great news, and it made them very happy. Jesus told them that they must go all over the world and tell people that God had come from heaven to live with people, that he loved them very much, that he died for them, but that he had come back from being dead. This good news would make people all over the world happy. When Jesus went to heaven he promised to come back again one day to take the people who love him to live in heaven with him. This is the good news, or gospel.

The four Gospel books were written by four different men named Matthew, Mark, Luke, and John.

Some people wonder why there are four Gospels. The reason is that we learn more about Jesus because four people saw different things when they were with Jesus and wrote down what they saw and heard. Suppose four children go to a birthday party. When they get home Mark tells his mom that they played pin-the-tail-on-the-donkey. Laurel tells her mom that they ate cake. Josh tells his mom about the presents, and Cheri tells her mom about the decorations. The four children were at the same party but different things about the party impressed each child. Matthew, Mark, Luke, and John all wrote about Jesus. They wrote different things, but all are true.

JOHN THE BAPTIST

When somebody important like a king or a president plans to visit a town, the people who live there get excited. They want their town to look nice and everything to be just right for the important visitor. So, before the guest arrives, a special planner goes to help the people get ready. Jesus was the most special visitor who ever went anywhere because he was God's Son. God wanted people to be ready for his arrival. The person God sent to help them get ready was named John.

John was not as important as Jesus but he was still very important. We know that because before John was born God sent an angel to John's father, Zechariah, to tell him that his wife, who was very old, was going to have a baby. The angel also said that the baby should be named John. Zechariah did not believe what the angel told him because he too was very old. So the angel said that Zechariah would not be able to speak until the baby was born.

When the baby was born everybody thought he would be called Zechariah after his father, but his mother said he was going to be called John. The people were surprised to hear this, so they asked his father, who still could not speak, "What is the baby's name?" Zechariah wrote on a tablet, "His name is John." As soon as Zechariah wrote this he was able to speak again, and the people knew that this baby called John was special.

John knew Jesus well because they were cousins. John also knew his job was to tell people that Jesus was God's Son, the most important person on earth ever, and they must get ready to welcome him. But many of the people were not interested, so John began to speak clearly

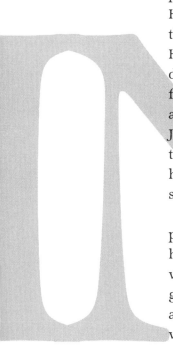

to them about the things they were doing that made God unhappy. Even though the people did not like what John was telling them, they still listened. John spoke to them out in the wilderness, and they walked long distances to hear what he had to say. As they listened, some of the people agreed John was right. They knew they were doing things that made God unhappy, and they were sorry.

John said if they were truly sorry they should be baptized. Then John used water to show how God would wash away people's sin in the same way that water washes away dirt and sand. People named him John the Baptist because he baptized so many people. One day Jesus asked John to baptize him. John didn't want to do it because he knew Jesus had never done anything wrong, but Jesus said that John must baptize him, so John did.

At the time John was telling the people to stop doing bad things, a powerful ruler in Israel named Herod was doing many wrong things. John was very brave and told Herod that he, too, should stop doing the bad things and get ready for God's Son Jesus. Herod became angry and told the soldiers to put John in prison. John still believed that Jesus was God's Son and that he had come to wash away people's sins.

One day Herod had a big birthday party, and a young girl danced for him. Herod was so pleased with what she did that he said he would give her anything she wanted. She asked her mother, who was Herod's wife, "What should I ask for?" Her

mother, who hated John, said, "Ask for John's head on a platter." This was a terrible thing to say, but Herod sent soldiers down to John's cell. They killed him and brought his head into the party on a platter.

Jesus said something very special about John. Jesus said that of all the men who were ever born, there was never a greater man than John the Baptist.

WHAT DOES **BAPTISM** MEAN?

IT COMES FROM A GREEK WORD WHICH MEANS "TO WASH."

Let's Pretend

SOLDIER SILVANUS

THIS STORY, TOLD HERE AS A FANTASY MARRIED TO FACT, IS TO BE MIXED WITH FAITH AND LAUGHTER, SHARED WITH LOVE AND JOY.

SOUNDS COMPLICATED TO ME. I'M JUST GOING TO ENJOY THE STORY

As Silvanus grew bigger he began to hang out with some rough boys who lived on the other side of town.

They did some bad things and got into trouble with the police. A kind judge said to Silvanus, "You are a big, bad, bad bully and you are going to get into serious trouble unless you change your ways. Young man, I think you should join the army, and they will teach you how to behave."

So Silvanus became a soldier. The army sent him away from home to the land of Palestine. Some of the soldiers there were kind to the people and the people liked them. But other soldiers treated the people unkindly. Silvanus, because he had learned to be rough with people and to do bad things when he was a boy, started to be unkind to the people. Instead of looking after them as he was supposed to, he began to take their money from them. When they complained, Strong-arm Soldier Silvanus said, "I deserve this extra money and I'm strong enough to take it from you. I don't want to be in your country. And I don't want to have to look after you people. And the army doesn't pay me enough money, either." He was tough and sometimes he even hit the people. If his officers had known about this he would have been punished. But Strong-arm Soldier Silvanus did the bad things only when nobody was watching.

One day his officer said to him, "Today, Silvanus, you and Tertius must go

Silvanus was a big boy, much bigger than other boys his age. He was not a nice young boy. He was rough with the other boys and girls. They were afraid of him because he was so big. They called him Strong-arm Silvanus because he was as mean as he was big. He never missed a chance to punch anyone who had something he wanted, or just because he felt like punching someone. Strong-arm Silvanus was a bully, a big, big bully.

21

out into the wilderness and see that there is no trouble among the crowds of people who are going there to listen to this man called John."

Silvanus knew that it was very hot in the wilderness and that it was a long march away. He didn't want to go, but he had to obey orders. "Sweat and sand and bugs. Bugs and sand and sweat. They don't pay me enough for this kind of work," he grumbled to Tertius. He added, "Who is this crazy man John, anyway?"

Silvanus soon found out. When he and Tertius came to the place where the great crowds were gathered, they saw John. Not much to look at. He was tall, very thin, with a long beard and piercing eyes. He wore rough clothes made of camel's hair. He used a wide leather belt to keep the clothes tied to him. But what a voice John had! It was loud, so loud everyone could clearly hear what he was saying. John was talking about God being unhappy with the way people were living. John talked about the bad things people were doing to each other. Some people were very unkind to the poor, they were selfish, always quarreling and fighting, and sometimes people stole money and other things from those who could not stop them. As Silvanus listened he thought that somebody had been telling John about him. Soldier Silvanus listened even more carefully. "God wants you to be sorry for the bad things you have done, to stop doing them, and to get ready for God's Son to forgive you and make you into a new person," John told the people.

Silvanus knew that John was telling the truth. So Silvanus went up to John, roughly pushing his way through the crowds because he was so big and looked so important in his uniform.

"Tell me, sir," he said to John, "what would somebody like me have to do to get ready for God's Son to change his life?"

John looked at him and said, "Mr. Soldier-man, you need to be sorry for being a bully, for the ways that you have been rough with people, sorry that you have never been satisfied with your wages and have taken other people's money. God is not pleased with the way you have been living. But he still loves you."

John said many more things to Silvanus. He told him that Jesus would take away all his sins, even those from when he was a young boy up until the time he became a rough soldier. And John said that God would give Silvanus a new heart and make him a good man, a brave soldier.

"But do I have to be baptized like all these other people?" asked the soldier.

"If you're really sorry and want God to change your life, you will be baptized to show that you mean it," John answered.

The crowd waited to hear what Soldier Silvanus would say. They knew he was a rough, tough, unkind man.

"John, you're right. I have done many wrong things and I'm sorry. I want God's Son to take away my sins. I want to get ready for him. Yes, I will be baptized," said Silvanus.

The people were overjoyed. John was happy. And Silvanus was beaming from ear to ear.

JOHN THE BAPTIST & ME

When a family gets ready for visitors, usually the house gets an extra good cleaning, some special things are baked or cooked for the visitors, and all the family members put on clean, fresh clothes. Sometimes flowers, candy, or other special things are put around the house to make the visitors feel welcome. How can we welcome Jesus into our hearts? John the Baptist, who wanted everyone to be ready for Jesus, said we have to do several things:

1. Stop doing bad things, such as lying, disobeying, complaining, being mean.
2. Be sorry for the bad things we've done.
3. Make up our minds that, with God's help, we'll never do those bad things again.
4. Believe that Jesus, God's Son, came to live on earth, died, and rose from the dead to pay for our sins.
5. Because we are now God's children, we'll try to do only things that please him.

25

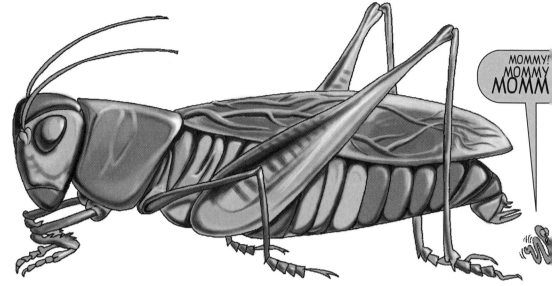

John the Baptist spent a lot of time preaching in the wilderness. He ate locusts and wild honey.

What is a locust?
an insect related to the grasshopper.
among the few insects clean that the Israelites were permitted to eat (Leviticus 11:21–22).

In some Middle East countries poor people still eat locusts. The head, legs, and wings are removed before locusts are boiled, stewed, roasted, or cooked in butter. Sometimes they are dried, salted, or eaten fresh without being cooked.

One of the ten plagues sent by the Lord on the Egyptians was a cloud of locusts that ate anything that was growing and green. The Egyptians believed locusts were sacred, or holy, so no one might kill a locust.

John probably found honeycombs in small spaces between rocks. Samson found honey in the carcass (dead body) of a lion.

Let's Make a Video about

PARTICIPANTS ARE ENCOURAGED TO **EXPAND** AND IMPROVISE, USING THIS MATERIAL AS A GUIDE. ALLOW YOUR IMAGINATION TO "PEEK AROUND THE CORNER OF THE VERSE" AND SEE WHO IS COMING.

WHY DO I HAVE THESE FANCY PANTS? I'M NOT A PARTICIPANT; I'M A SPECTATOR.

Your Family Video Theater

The Angel

Cast: Zechariah, Elizabeth

Scene: Zechariah, an old man, comes into the room where his wife, Elizabeth, is sitting.

Elizabeth	Welcome home, Zechariah. I've missed you while you were away serving as a priest in the temple. But I know you've wanted to do this all your life, and finally your once-in-a-lifetime opportunity came! Tell me all about it!
Zechariah	*(pointing to his mouth and shaking his head)* Mmm. Mmm.
Elizabeth	*(laughing)* Come on, you old tease, tell me what happened.
Zechariah	*(shaking his head more violently)* Mm. Mmmm.
Elizabeth	Whatever is the matter? Have you lost your speech?
Zechariah	*(nodding his head)* Mmm. Mmm.
Elizabeth	Did you catch a cold?
Zechariah	*(points to his eyes, which are wide open)* Mmm. Mmm.
Elizabeth	You saw something?
Zechariah	*(nodding enthusiastically)* Mmm. Mmm.
Elizabeth	What did you see that would make you lose your speech?
Zechariah	*(spreads his arms wide, sticks out his chest, stands very still)*
Elizabeth	A bird, a big bird? You saw a bird that frightened you?
Zechariah	*(shakes his head from side to side, points to the sky, brings his arms down in a fluttering motion, and then stands tall and still)* Mmm. Mmm.

Elizabeth	An angel? Are you saying you saw an angel? I don't believe it.
Zechariah	*(nods, pleased that Elizabeth has finally understood him)*
Elizabeth	Are you sure? Why would an angel come to you?
Zechariah	*(points to himself and then to Elizabeth, crosses his arms as if holding a baby, and begins to rock quietly while humming in a monotone "Rock-a-bye Baby")*
Elizabeth	The angel told you someone was going to have a baby?
Zechariah	*(nods and smiles, pointing again at himself and then Elizabeth)*
Elizabeth	You don't mean we are going to have a baby! Are you crazy?
Zechariah	*(nods even more earnestly)* Mmm. Mmm.
Elizabeth	At our age? That's ridiculous. You didn't see an angel. You had a nightmare! You stayed too long in the sun. You ate cheese before going to bed.
Zechariah	*(looking sad, shakes his head and then stands like a preacher, waves his arms, and pretends to be speaking to a large group of people, then acts as if people are listening and crying and then being baptized, all the time nodding his head and looking earnestly at Elizabeth.)* Mmm. Mmm.
Elizabeth	He's going to be a preacher? Crowds are going to listen to him? They're going to repent and be baptized? I never heard of such a thing! Is that what you're saying?
Zechariah	*(nods again, looks hopefully at his wife)* Mmm. Mmm.
Elizabeth	*(laughs and shakes her head)* Next you'll be telling me he told you what to call the baby!
Zechariah	*(stoops down and and with his finger begins to write in the dust on the table J O H N)*
Elizabeth	This is too much. You're saying the angel told you we would have a baby who would become a great preacher and his name would be John? *(adds in a mocking tone)* I suppose he also told you the boy would be the Messiah!
Zechariah	*(shakes his head from side to side, then with his left hand makes two fingers move like walking and with the right hand does the same thing. The two hands suggest one person walking after the other)* Mmm. Mmm.
Elizabeth	He won't be the Messiah, but he will walk before him? Is that what you're trying to say?

Zechariah	*(nods again, looking happy that Elizabeth is getting the message)* Mmm. Mmm.
Elizabeth	It's too amazing to believe. But we did pray for years that we would have a baby. Is God going to give us a special boy? The one who will prepare the way for the Savior? I just can't wait to tell my cousin Mary.
Zechariah	*(raises his hands, nods vigorously, eyes shining)* Mmm. Mmm.

JESUS IS BORN AND GROWS UP

When it was time for Jesus to come to earth so he could save the people from their sins, God sent his angel Gabriel to tell a young girl named Mary that God had chosen her as the mother of Jesus. Her baby would be different from any other baby in the whole world, for God, rather than a man, would be his father. Mary was surprised that God had chosen her to have a part in this wonderful thing that was about to happen, but she told God she would be happy to do all that he wanted her to do.

At first Joseph, Mary's fiancé, didn't understand why she was having a baby in this amazing way, and he wanted to call off the wedding. Joseph said Mary's story was hard to believe, and so did other people in the village where she lived. Then God spoke to Joseph in a dream and explained that everything Mary had

told him was true. Mary was going to have the most special baby that had ever been born. He was to be great and would be called the Son of the Most High. His human name would be Jesus, which means Savior, because his life work would be to save people from going to hell, which they deserve, and take them to heaven instead.

God told other people, such as Zechariah, who was married to Elizabeth, Mary's cousin, about this plan.

Almost a year later, Mary and Joseph had to go to Bethlehem to fill out some forms. The Roman government had told everyone they must register in the town in which they had been born, and that is why Joseph brought Mary to Bethlehem, the town where he had been born. While they were looking for a place to stay, Mary told Joseph that the

baby was about to be born. Joseph didn't know what to do because all the places to stay were full. Then a kind innkeeper let them use the cattle shed at the back of the inn. This place wasn't the best place for a baby to be born, but it was a shelter that kept them warm. God was so happy Jesus came into the world to show people how to be forgiven for their sins. He wanted his angels to sing about it. A heavenly choir of many, many angels sang in the sky above Bethlehem.

The people who stayed out all night were shepherds guarding their sheep, and they saw and heard the angel choir sing about the baby. They hurried to town to see what it was all about.

The shepherds couldn't believe Jesus was staying in a cattle shed when he had come from heaven and was the Son of God. But they knew he was the baby the angels had told them about because the angels had said the baby would be lying in a feeding trough, and that's exactly where they saw him. The shepherds were so excited they told everyone what the angels had said about the baby and how he had come to earth to be the Savior of the world.

While Jesus was still a baby, the wise men came to find him. They followed the star God had sent to guide them to Israel. They first stopped in Jerusalem where King Herod lived in a very big palace. They asked Herod if he knew exactly where they could find the young boy who would be king someday. King Herod was afraid the boy would become king instead of him or his son but he pretended he

wanted to find Jesus and worship him too. Herod quickly called his helpers and told them to find out more information about a star that would announce that a king had been born. The helpers found the answer. The baby would be born in Bethlehem. So Herod sent the wise men to Bethlehem to search for the little boy. Herod told them to let him know where Jesus was so he also could come and worship.

King Herod really wanted to kill Jesus. When the wise men—having been warned by an angel not to report back to the wicked king— didn't come back to Jerusalem, the king sent soldiers to Bethlehem to kill all the little boys under the age of two. This way he was sure he could get rid of his rival. The soldiers did what King Herod told them to do.

How cruel and terrible this was! The mothers and fathers cried, and the brothers and sisters and grandmas and grandpas of the little boys who were murdered wept. Herod's soldiers did not get Jesus. The very night before this terrible thing happened, an angel told Joseph and Mary to take Jesus and run away to Egypt.

After a while God's angel told Mary and Joseph that King Herod was dead and it was safe to come back home. Joseph brought the family back to their hometown, Nazareth, and settled down. Jesus grew up in Nazareth. He helped Joseph in his carpenter shop. The Bible says Jesus grew up to be a strong young man.

Jesus was the same as us, but different. He was God, but he was a man too. There never has been any-one like him before, nor will there ever be anyone like him again. The way he was born, the way he lived, the way he died, the way he was alive again and went to heaven, were all very different, very special, for he was the perfect Son of God who came to do the most important work anyone ever did.

Let's Pretend

ANNA & SIMEON

Anna had a cold. She felt terrible. She didn't feel like getting up and going out into the temple courtyard. She had been up till the early hours of the morning pray-ing. Maybe she shouldn't stay up so late now that she was so old. *I must be the oldest person in the whole temple,* she thought. She laughed to herself. Maybe she was. She was eighty-four.

But she loved to be there among God's things and his people. When her husband

had died many years before, she had begun to serve God night and day in the temple, hardly ever leaving. There was plenty of work to do and lots of time to sing and pray and enjoy worshiping God. Anna had a special way of knowing what God wanted to say to people. He would tell her the message, and she would tell the people. They knew about Anna and came for her blessing and advice. Because of this, Anna had lots of friends. Simeon was one of them. He was very old too. He loved and served God as much as Anna did.

Anna got up and dressed even though it was still very early. Today Simeon was com-ing to talk with her, and that would be spe-cial. Anna looked forward to their talks to-gether about the Lord. She went out into the large temple courtyard. Some women with their husbands and babies were there already. Most of the babies were only eight days old, which was the age to present them to the Lord at the temple. Parents usually gave an offering in thankful-ness for the baby's safe arrival.

"Pigeons and doves for sale!" called out a little boy named Jacob who had cages

full of birds he was selling. Every day he brought pigeons and doves to the temple. His father raised the birds, and Jacob sold them to the temple worshipers to use as offerings.

One day Jacob had asked his father, "Why do people buy two pigeons or two doves for an offering?" His father had explained that God's law said it was the right thing to do. It was good to do exactly what God said was the right thing to do. Jacob knew that rich people bought more expensive animals for offerings and that the very poor people could afford

only the pigeons and doves. He was a poor boy himself, but he made a little money from the sale of birds to give to his father to help feed their large family.

Anna greeted Jacob warmly. She was fond of the young boy. "Shalom," she said. That was the word people used to greet each other in Israel.

"Shalom, Anna," Jacob replied respectfully. He loved the old woman who always stopped to talk to him. Sometimes when business was slow she would sit by him and tell him wonderful stories about God's people and the adventures they had had in olden times. She would *always* say something about
the Messiah—

the Lord's Christ who had been promised by the prophets. He would come one day to save the world.

"When do you think he will come?" Jacob asked her this day.

"At the right time," Anna answered. "Maybe when you are a man, Jacob. But then again he might even come today!"

Jacob jumped and looked around. "What would we do if he just came walking right up to us?" he asked Anna. "How would we know it was him? Would he look like a great king? Would he have shiny clothes like they say the angels wear? How will we know him?"

"We'll know, Jacob," she said softly. Anna smiled down at him. "We'll know. God will tell us."

Anna turned to greet a mother and her husband. The girl looked no older than a young teenager. She held an eight-day-old baby closely to her. Her eyes shone with pride and joy. Anna smiled. She loved to see such mothers delighting in their little ones. She had a special heart for children. The father was choosing two young pigeons for a thank offering for the baby. Jacob noticed his hands: strong and worn with work. This man was poor like Jacob, but he had a wonderful smile. Jacob liked him and asked where he had come from. The man took time to talk with the small boy. Anna had seen Simeon come into the temple and went to greet him. Then she turned to talk to some visitors while Simeon approached the young couple who were with Jacob.

"Shalom, Simeon," Jacob greeted him, but Simeon didn't seem to hear. His eyes were fixed on the baby boy in the young girl's arms.

Jacob worried about the way Simeon looked. Everyone knew he was sick. Some people said he had only weeks to live, but the old man was telling everyone God had promised him he wouldn't die until he saw the Lord's Christ, the promised Savior of the world. "Old people can get a little funny in the head," Jacob murmured to his doves and pigeons.

But now Simeon had the baby in his arms and was almost dancing around with joy. His eyes sparkled

and his smile was as wide as his face. The young parents were staring at him. Suddenly Simeon began to praise God and talk to him out loud. People gathered around. They knew that old Simeon lived very close to God; they really respected him and wanted to hear what he had to say.

"Lord," he prayed, "you promised I would not die until I had seen your salvation. My eyes have seen it! This child is a light for the whole world." The parents stood by with their mouths open as Simeon blessed their baby and talked to them about what was ahead.

Jacob stood on his tiptoes, straining to see the little baby in Simeon's arms. Simeon, aware of the boy, knelt down to show the baby to him. Jacob looked and looked at the baby Jesus. This tiny little person was the Messiah? The Lord's Christ? How could he be? Why, his parents were poor just like Jacob's. The baby was wrapped in common swaddling bands, no royal robe. And he was so little, so fragile. Would God come to them in such helplessness? What if his mother dropped him or he got sick? What if he was kidnapped by wicked men?

Looking up, Jacob saw Anna at her friend Simeon's side. Simeon stood up to greet her. Before Simeon said anything Anna took the baby and started telling the people who were gathered around them that this was the child who had come from God to save them from their sins. He had come to bring his kingdom to earth.

Jacob could not believe his ears. Turning, he ran to the bird cage and hurriedly took out two of his best pigeons. He quickly put them into Joseph's hands.

"Please, sir, take them. Please. They are a gift for the baby. They are *my* gift of thankfulness. I believe what Simeon and Anna have said is true, for all of us know that these old people are God's mouthpiece and speak only what is from him. I have seen God's Son with my own eyes today! I have touched his little fingers. I can live now, knowing that God has actually come into our world, just like one of us!"

Joseph thanked the little boy for his gift—a gift Joseph knew had cost Jacob dearly. Taking the pigeons, Joseph, Mary, Simeon, and Anna walked toward the priest at the end of the courtyard. Jacob's heart sang. Jacob's eyes danced. Jacob's life would never be the same again. Jacob had seen God!

JESUS & ME

What will you do by the time you are twelve years old? Lots of things. You'll go to school starting in kindergarten, play hundreds of different games with your sisters and brothers and friends, do hours and hours of homework, eat thousands of meals, and take many different sorts of vacations.

Before Jesus was twelve years of age he had done all the things you have done too. He just did them many years ago, in another place, in another way. But he knows what it feels like to be a baby, a child, and a young person.

STUFF Neat stuff Nea

Often in Palestine when a baby was born local musicians met at the house to greet with simple music the baby's arrival into the world. Many, many angels sang when Christ was born!

We name the years before Christ was born **B.C.** (before Christ). After he came to earth we started over again with 1 and put **A.D.** before the number. The letters **A.D.** are the abbreviation for two Latin words *anno Domini* ([AH-NO DOE-MEH-NEE] in the year of our Lord). Someone made a colossal error, or big mistake. Actually **A.D. 1** should have begun two years earlier. Christ came to earth two years before the calendar numbers were changed. So the year we celebrate as 2000 is really 2002.

When one of God's angels told Mary and Joseph to go to Egypt, they left in a hurry. They were like refugees and could take only the things they absolutely needed and could carry with them. They had no idea how much time they would spend in Egypt. If you had to leave your home and had ten minutes to choose only the things you could

carry in one suitcase, what would you take? You would have to walk because you could not take a car or bike or roller blades. You would be going to a place where you knew no one, had no relatives, probably had no place to live, could not understand the language, and where your father and mother had no jobs.

Let's Make a Video about

PARTICIPANTS ARE ENCOURAGED TO EXPAND AND IMPROVISE, USING THIS MATERIAL AS A GUIDE. ALLOW YOUR IMAGINATION TO "PEEK AROUND THE CORNER OF THE VERSE" AND SEE WHO IS "COMING."

QUICK! HELP ME FIND THE CORNER.

Your Family Video Theater

Lost in the Temple

Cast: *Mother (Mary), Father (Joseph), Jesus, John, Jude, James, Ben, Lazarus, Martha, Hannah, two teachers*

Scene: *On the road from Jerusalem to Nazareth*

Narrator	When Jesus was twelve years of age, he went with his family to Jerusalem for a feast. When it was over, Joseph and Mary and all their relatives began the long journey home.
Mother	Come on, James and John, stop squabbling. We have a long way to go.
James	Are we nearly there?
Mother	No, we're *not* nearly there. We have another whole day to go.
John	But it's hot. May I ride the donkey?
Father	Rachel is too little to walk far. She needs the donkey. Shape up now, boys, and keep going.
Lazarus	I like going to the temple, but I don't like getting there and back. My legs ache.
Martha	But it's so much fun. Everyone comes, and we have such happy times together. It's great being with all the cousins, uncles, and aunts.
Mother	Joseph, have you seen Jesus?
Father	Not since we left the city early this morning. I thought he was with James and John.
Mother	So did I, but I just saw them, and he wasn't with them. Hannah! Hannah, have you seen Jesus anywhere?
Hannah	Not since this morning.
James	Are we nearly there?

Father	James, stop that! Have you seen Jesus? I thought he was with you.
James	Not since early this morning. *(He runs over to his brother Jude.)* Jude, have you seen Jesus? The oldest brother of ours has gone and got himself lost. It's not like him. He's always doing the right thing. Now he's got Mother and Father really worried because they thought he was with us or one of the relatives.
Jude	But where could he be? I hope nothing's happened to him. There are all sorts of thieves and robbers around on these special feast days.
James	Jesus can look after himself. I'm not worried about him. I just don't want to go back to look for him.
Jude	Go back! Oh! No! It's a long walk as it is.
Mother	*(to Father)* Joseph, we need to send the other children on with Hannah and go back to Jerusalem to look for Jesus ourselves. We thought that he was with our friends and family but for the whole day he has been lost.
Hannah	I'll be glad to take the children home. You'd better go back right now. Something must have happened to him. It's not like Jesus to cause you any trouble. There must be a reason.

Scene: In Jerusalem

Narrator	So Mary and Joseph returned to Jerusalem to look for Jesus. They searched for three days and were getting desperate.
Father	Maybe he was with our group after all, and we missed him. Perhaps we should go on home. Who knows? Maybe we'll find him safe and sound. *(stopping a small boy)* Hey, Ben, I saw you in the temple—remember us? You were talking to Jesus. He's your age.
Ben	Yes, sir, I remember you. And I remember your son. I wanted him to stay on so we could be friends.
Mother	Have you seen him, Ben?
Ben	Why yes, I just left him on the temple porch.
Father	The temple! Of course! Why didn't we go there *first?* How his face lit up to be in the house of God!
Mother	And his twelve-year-old interest in all things to do with the law and the prophets. Why didn't we think of looking for him in the temple right away!

Narrator	*(action behind)* Mary and Joseph quickly thanked Ben as they hurried away in the direction of the temple.

Scene: A corner in the temple

Narrator	Sure enough, they found Jesus sitting among the teachers, listening to them and asking them questions.
Mother	Son! Why have you treated us like this? Your father and I have been searching for you all over Jerusalem for the last three days.
Father	We have been really worried.
Jesus	Why were you searching for me in the city? Didn't you know I had to be in my Father's house?
Father	I don't really understand why you had to be here. We have been looking everywhere for you. It's time to go home.
Teacher 1	Your son has a great understanding of the things to do with God, sir. You should be very proud of him.
Teacher 2	We have been amazed at his answers to our questions.
Father	Sirs, thank you for your instruction, but we must go now. We are already three days late returning home.
Narrator	Mary and Joseph did not understand why it was so important for Jesus to be in his Father God's house. Perhaps they were not thinking about what a special child he was and what he had come to do. The Bible says that Jesus went back to Nazareth with his parents and was obedient to them.
Mother	*(praying)* Oh, Lord, help me to treasure in my heart and understand all these things that your son, your dear son, says and does.
Narrator	Jesus grew in wisdom and stature (that probably means height, but it could also mean value) and in favor with God and men.

Today is Christ the Lord in the born to a Savior David town of has been Luke you; 2:11

Grow Like Jesus

Words and Music by
JILL BRISCOE and LARRY MOORE

Je - sus

1. grew   in strength and pow'r,   wi - ser   by the day, the hour.____
2. for - ests that he had made,   Je - sus   grew in skill - ful trade.____
3. grew   to know God's law,   al - ways seek - ing, want - ing more.____

Pleas - ing those who knew his love._____ Smiled u - pon by God a - bove Je- sus grew.
Worked a work - day, earned his pay._____ Wear - ied by the end of the day.
Set his heart to do God's will._____ Through trials and trou - bles, trust - ed still

I will too._____ I can

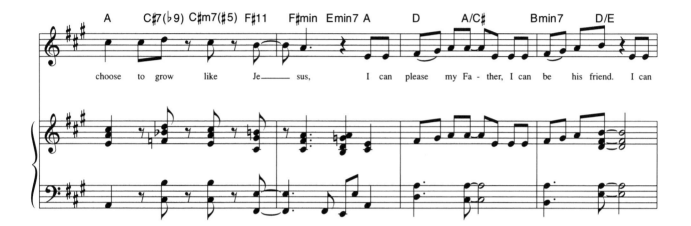

choose to grow like Je——sus, I can please my Fa - ther, I can be his friend. I can

choose to grow like Je——sus, I can serve him on - ly to the end. Je-sus grew.

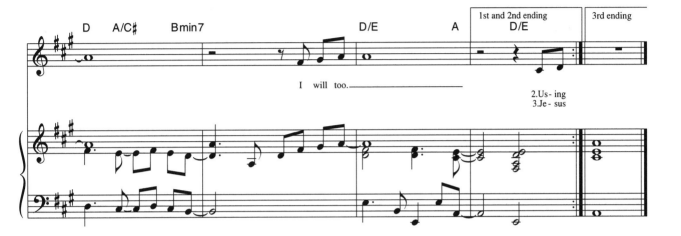

I will too.————————

2.Us- ing
3.Je - sus

JESUS HEALS AND HELPS AND TEACHES

Jesus loved to tell people about his Father in heaven. The people wanted to learn about God but did not always understand. Jesus knew how to talk about difficult things in such a clear way that even the children could know what he was talking about. One day he talked to the people on a hillside overlooking the beautiful Sea of Galilee. Men and women and boys and girls gathered around him as he sat on the grass and began to talk to them.

"I know that you are worried about many things. But you shouldn't worry," Jesus said. Some of the people wondered how they could stop worrying, because they had many problems. Jesus said that his Father knew about their problems and he would care for them.

Somebody in the crowd shouted out, "Master, you can say that we should not worry, but how do we know that the Father will look after us? I have four children at home and I have to feed them. What will happen if I can't get enough food for them?"

Just as he said this a tiny bird flew overhead and settled on the branch of a tree. It stayed there for a few minutes, very quietly, almost as if it were listening to what Jesus was saying. Jesus saw the quiet bird and said, "Well, look at this bird. The Father looks after him, doesn't he? If he cares about the bird, surely he will care for you!" The people smiled, and the man who had asked the question seemed to be helped by the answer too.

Jesus went on to say, "Some of you worry about what you're going to wear."

"That's right," said a woman in the crowd. "I have been invited to a wedding and I don't have special clothes."

49

how does Jesus help me stop worrying?

Jesus didn't seem concerned. He didn't have many nice clothes either, but he had been to a wedding dressed as he was, and it had been all right. Jesus knew the lady was worried, so he got up, walked toward her, stooped down, and picked a pretty flower that was growing at her feet. He gave it to her and said, "Now look at this flower. Isn't it beautiful? Hasn't the Father clothed this little flower, which will live only a few days?"

Taking the flower from him the woman said, "Yes, it is beautiful, and the Father has made it beautiful."

"Well, then," said Jesus, "you are much more important than the flower, so the Father will make sure you look beautiful too when you need to."

The people gathered around Jesus were happy to hear his words.

"But, Master!" someone in the crowd shouted out. "We are poor people. We don't have much money, and life is hard for us."

"I know," said Jesus, "I don't have much money either. But let me tell you something. When you save lots of money you worry about where to keep it and how to make sure that thieves don't steal it. If you buy things with it you worry about what will happen to the things you buy. But if you think about working for heavenly things no one can steal them, and they won't rust in the rain, and moths won't eat them." The people laughed when he said that, because they knew it wouldn't rain in heaven and there wouldn't be any moths flying around. They liked that.

"You really must learn to trust your heavenly Father, and if you do, you'll be able to help other people."

"How can we help other people?" a young boy in the crowd asked.

Pointing away to the left, Jesus said, "Look at this village sitting on top of the hill. You see the gleaming white buildings? Now, when you are out on the lake in your fishing boat and a storm comes, how do you know where you are?"

An old fisherman said, "I look for the village sitting on the hill. It is always there and it helps me know where I am."

"That's right," said Jesus. "And when you learn to trust the Father and stop worrying, people will look to you to see how they should live their lives too."

Jesus told the people many more things, and they remembered them. Each time they saw a bird or a flower or looked at the village on the hill they thought about what he had said and they learned to trust and not to worry.

50

Let's Pretend

FLYING FISH and the FOUR FEET

Flying Fish hurled himself through the water, burst through the surface, and enjoyed the warm air and sunlight that touched his wet scales for a brief moment before he plunged into the water again. He laughed with sheer delight and thanksgiving to the one who had made him a flying fish. So few fish could do what he did! Others could do things he couldn't do, but none could fly through the air easily, jumping and bouncing over the surface winds on the face of the Sea of Galilee. Sometimes he was able to see how the fishermen's boats looked above the water instead of how the fish saw

EEEEW! OW! I JUST STEPPED ON A "BE"

them from below the surface. Not that he wanted to see very much of them. He knew how dangerous the fishermen's nets might be to him and his family.

This day, however, there were no boats in sight. Maybe that had to do with the clouds he noticed that were beginning to gather. "A storm is coming," Flying Fish told his family. "We need to be careful. It will be hard to fly through the pounding waves and spray when the storm begins."

"Well, one good thing about a storm," said Frying Fish, his uncle, "is that there won't be any fishermen out to catch us."

The water on the surface began to churn and boil, and the school of flying fish dove a little deeper for comfort. The water darkened as the sky above blackened and the rain slashed down. The storm was bad.

Suddenly Frying Fish shouted, "Look above us!" All the little fish looked up to the surface of the water. Big oars and the bottom of a fishing boat appeared. The boat was being tossed this way and that, and the oars were going in all directions.

"What are they doing out in this mess?" asked Father Flying Fish in amazement. "They are right in the middle of the lake, far from land, and everyone knows how terrible these storms can be."

"They'll never make it across the lake," Frying Fish worried out loud.

"I wonder who's in the boat? I know; I'll just fly up and see," said Flying Fish. Before anyone could stop him he had leaped high into the air to find out.

The men in the boat, disciples of Jesus, were very frightened. Jesus was not with them. He had told them to get into the boat and go ahead of him. They lived on the other side of the lake and had no idea how Jesus was going to get home, as it took almost a day to walk around the lake. But the men had no time to worry about that now. The storm was so terrible they wondered if they would ever get home alive.

Flying Fish saw their big eyes wide with fear, saw the high waves, and heard the thunder. He swam down into the water to report what was happening. The fish began to swim around the boat to watch the oars. The boat rocked and bucked like a horse out of control.

Suddenly Father Flying Fish let out a fish gurgle (like a fish scream). All the fish looked up to the surface of the water to where he was pointing with his flying fin.

There, as clear as could be, were two feet *walking* on the top of the water. "Two feet!" bubbled Flying Fish. "Two feet! Who . . . who do they belong to?"

"And why don't the feet sink into the water?" bubbled Father Flying Fish.

Flying Fish quickly swam up to the surface of the water, launched himself into the air, and found himself face to face with his creator. Jesus of Nazareth was the owner of those two feet the fish had seen walking on the water.

Flying Fish was so dumbfounded he fell like a stone back into the sea and could hardly burble out his report to the others.

"You mean it's Jesus?" Mother Flying Fish asked in a faint fishy way. "Our Jesus, the fish maker?"

"Yes, yes, yes," Flying Fish burbled back, "Our Jesus! And you should have seen the look on the men's faces. They thought they were seeing a ghost!"

The fish laughed as they swam up to the surface to see for themselves. As they burst through the waves together, leaping high in the air, they heard a big man—someone called him Peter—say, "Lord, if it's really you, tell me to come to you on the water." Now the fish were back in the depths, but not before some of them had heard Jesus tell the men not to be afraid.

"I heard him say 'Come' to Peter," Frying Fish said excitedly.

"Look! Look up there," whispered Father Flying Fish. The fish looked. Now they were looking at the soles of four feet! Peter had gotten out of the boat to go to Jesus.

Things happened next so quickly the little flying fish circling the scene could hardly keep up with it all. Peter looked at the storm instead of at Jesus and forgot to trust Jesus to keep him walking on the water. As soon as Peter did this, he began to sink. The little fish saw the body of the big fisherman sink in the tossing waves, but then they heard him cry a great cry, "Lord, save me!"

Down into the water came the hands of Jesus. He grasped Peter firmly by his clothes and yanked him out of the sea. Flying Fish made a last jump just in time to

hear Jesus say to Peter, "You of little faith,
why did you doubt?"

The fish watched the four feet walk
back to the boat and disappear as they
got inside.

"Hey, have you noticed something?"
Frying Fish gasped.

"Yes," said Father Flying Fish, "the sea
has become calm. The storm is over."

The men in the boat were worshiping
the Lord Jesus. "Truly, you are the Son of
God," Flying Fish heard them say.

"Why did it take so long for those men
to understand that?" Flying Fish wondered. "We knew at once who those feet
belonged to, and we are just fish."

The little fish never forgot that wonderful time on the Sea of Galilee. Ever since,
some fish have been jumping and flying
out of the water hoping they might see
Jesus again.

JESUS & ME

Isn't it great to know that the Lord Jesus knows how we feel about things? About *everything!* How do we know he knows? We know because he visited our world. Sometimes we don't feel like going to Sunday school. Jesus went to Sunday school—except it was Saturday school because the Jews had their Sabbath on Saturday. Some people today have their Sabbath on Saturday too.

Sometimes he probably wished he didn't have to go to church with all the other people, you don't want to do? Do they tell you to do things like clean your bedroom, hang up your clothes, take out the garbage? There were times when Joseph, Jesus' father, must have asked him to do things he didn't want to do. But we know he did them because God wanted him to—and he did them with a smile.

Many of Jesus' disciples were fishermen before they left their jobs to be with Jesus. The two sons of Zebedee, James and John, were fishing when Jesus called them to be disciples. Peter and Andrew were fishermen too.

Fishing on the Sea of Galilee was not done with a hook and line and bait like we use today. The men who fished the Sea of Galilee used nets. One type of net was small and round and was thrown into the water from the shore or from shallow water and then hauled in with its catch of fish.

Sometimes a dragnet (a long piece of net shaped like a giant-size loaf of bread) was tied between two boats or between one boat on the water and fishermen walking along the shore. The net was slowly pulled through the water. We know some of the disciples had boats and may have used dragnets on occasion.

THOSE POOR FISH! WHAT ARE THEY GONNA DO WITH ALL THOSE FISH? WHERE WILL THEY TAKE THEM?

WILL ALL OF THEM FIT ON THE BOAT? OR WILL THEY SINK THE BOAT?

After the net was on the shore, fishermen sorted the catch of fish and tossed away the fish that Jews were forbidden to eat—fish such as eels, shellfish, or anything that did not have fins and scales.

Because Jesus was the Son of God, he had power that ordinary people do not have. He used his power to do many good things when he lived on earth. We call those acts *miracles*. The Bible does not tell us about all the miracles Jesus did. These are just a few of them.

Power over Water

- Made a storm stop—Luke 8:22–25
- Walked on the water—Mark 6:45–52
- Helped Peter get a large catch of fish—Luke 5:1–11
- Put a catch of 153 big fish in the disciples' net—John 21:1–14
- Put money in the first fish Peter caught one day—Matthew 17:24–27

Power over Food

- Turned water into wine—John 2:1–11
- Fed 5,000 people bread and fish—Matthew 14:15–21
- Fed 4,000 people bread and fish—Mark 8:1–9
- Made a fig tree dry up—Matthew 21:17–22

Power over Sickness

- Healed men with bad skin disease (leprosy)—Matthew 8:1–4
- Healed a paralyzed man—Mark 2:1–12
- Healed several blind men—Matthew 20:29–34; Mark 8:22–26; John 9:1–41
- Healed a woman who could not stand straight—Luke 13:10–17 Healed a man with very large arms and legs—Luke 14:1–6
- Healed people who could not hear or speak—Mark 7:31–37
- Healed a man who had his ear cut off—John 18:10–11

Power over Death

These people were dead and Jesus made them alive again:

- Young girl—Mark 5:35–43
- Young boy—Luke 7:11–17
- Lazarus—John 11:1–44

Fancy Footnotes

WHAT DOES **WORRIED** MEAN?

THAT'S JUST ANOTHER WAY OF SAYIN"...

YOU'RE **SCARED!**

Let's Make a Video about

Cast: Syc, Zac, boy, girl, Zeb and Jeb (two men from Jericho), Buzzy Bee

Scene: Street in front of Zaccheus's house.

Narrator	Jericho was a lovely city. Beyond its farms was wilderness where little grew, but Jericho had lots of water with trees and parks. In one part of town a family of sycamore trees grew alongside one of the main roads. The people loved to gather under the trees in the heat of the day because the leaves gave lots of cool shade. When one of the trees was quite young some boys had damaged it so that it did not grow to its full height. Everybody knew this tree because it looked different standing so short among the taller trees.
Boy	We can't call this tree a sycamore because it's only half a tree. Let's call it Syc.
Syc	I'm so embarrassed. My leaves are turning red because they feel ashamed of my name. Maybe just once someone could call me by my real name.
Narrator	Right behind where Syc grew was a large house. In this house lived a very rich man. But nobody liked him. He had become rich by working as a chief tax collector. Zac not only worked for the Romans, he also charged the people too much and kept the difference for himself. Every day he became richer and richer.
Zeb	I sure hate to pay the high taxes that little Zac charges us. He keeps so much for himself.
Jeb	Look at the nice clothes he wears. And his house is so large. Four families could easily live in it. He's overcharging us poor people to pay for all that stuff.
Zeb	I never did trust that little man, did you?

Jeb	No, every time I pay taxes I get mad at him. He just looks up and grins because he knows I have to pay what he tells me to.
Zac	*(leaving house)* Good morning, Friend Syc.
Syc	*(fluttering his leaves)* Good morning, Zac. *(muttering to himself)* I know how Zac feels about being so short. He isn't tall enough for folks to call him by his full name *Zaccheus.*
Girl	Do you know what's happening today in Jericho?
Boy	I heard that Jesus is coming. That's why everyone is pushing and shoving and lining the streets to get a good spot to see him.
Zeb	Go away, Zac, we don't want you standing in the front line.
Jeb	Get out of the way, Shorty. We were here first.
Zac	I wish people liked me. I really want to see Jesus today. But nobody here will let me get close to the front and I'm too short to see over people. I might as well go home.
Syc	*(waving branches)* Zac, you look sad. Do you want to watch for Jesus from one of my branches?
Zac	That's a good idea, Syc. You are the only friend I have.
Syc	Ouch! Watch what you're doing with your big feet.
Zac	Sorry. I've got such big feet and short legs. I wonder why God made me that way. I'll just pull some of these branches apart so I can see what's going on.
Syc	Be careful! Don't knock off any of my leaves.
Zac	Oh, don't worry about that. Even if I knock off a few leaves, you've got plenty left.
Syc	Very funny. It will be a long time before I let you use my branches again.
Buzzy Bee	Out of my way. What's your nose doing touching the flower I want to land on? Can't you see I'm buzzy?
Zac	Can't you see I'm busy too? I don't like bees, especially bees who buzz around my nose.
Jeb	Who is Zac talking to?
Boy	He must be talking to that bee. There's nobody else in there.
Zeb	Bee? That could never be. Be quiet. Bee indeed! Talking to a bee!
Jeb	To bee or not to bee, that is the question.

Narrator	Just then Jesus and his friends came walking by and every-body forgot about Zac and Syc and Buzzy.
Buzzy	I need to get that pollen. I hope Zac doesn't move his nose. If he does, I'll sting him. Here goes—
Zac	I need to move just a little bit close to that flower so I can see Jesus. Oh, oh! Buzzy landed on my nose. I'll just slap him away *(slaps at nose three times)*. Ouch, Ouch, OUCH!! Buzzy stung me right on the top of my nose.
Narrator	Jesus heard the commotion, looked up into the tree, and said, "There you are Zaccheus. I've been looking for you. I want to go to your house today. Come down out of that tree."
Zac	How can I get down fast? Syc will complain if I scrape some of his bark or make him lose some leaves. I'll have to be fast and careful. Whoops, I almost fell out of the tree. There, one more branch to go and I can jump to the ground.
Narrator	All the people were quiet as they watched Jesus and Zac walk toward Zac's house. Zac looked much taller as he walked with Jesus. Syc didn't mind that he lost a few leaves and some of his bark. And Buzzy, well, he just went back to being a bee.

You are the Son of the living Christ, the God. Matthew 16:16

IF YOU UNSCRAMBLE THE WORDS, ITS PRETTY AND POWERFUL— LIKE SUNSHINE.

OOOOOOH!!!! THAT'S A PRETTY ONE!

The Sower and the Seed

Words and Music by
JILL BRISCOE and LARRY MOORE

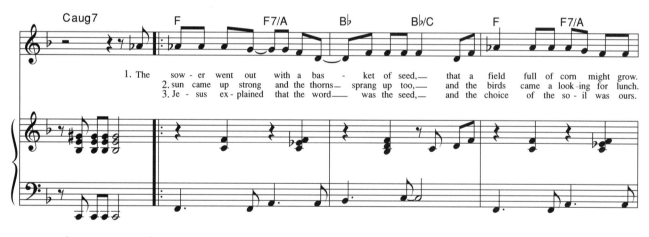

1. The sow-er went out with a bas-ket of seed,— that a field full of corn might grow.
2. sun came up strong and the thorns— sprang up too,— and the birds came a look-ing for lunch.
3. Je-sus ex-plained that the word— was the seed,— and the choice of the so-il was ours.

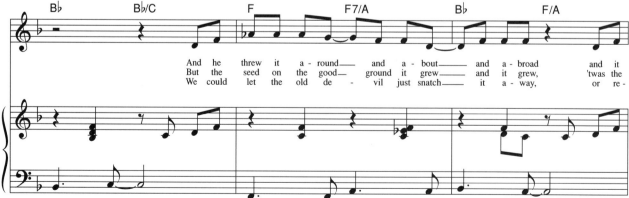

And he threw it a-round— and a-bout— and a-broad and it
But the seed on the good— ground it grew— and it grew, 'twas the
We could let the old de-vil just snatch— it a-way, or re-

land ed all o - ver the show. And it land-ed all o - ver the show.
seed on the path that was munched! 'Twas the seed on the path that was munched!
sist him with all of our powr's, Or re - sist him with all of our powr's.

And some fell on good ground, and some fell on the thorns, and
The thorns choked the good ness right out of the rest, and the
We could let all our wor ries just stran gle the seed, we could

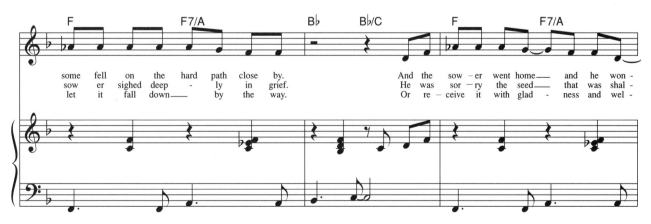

some fell on the hard path close by. And the sow - er went home and he won -
sow er sighed deep - ly in grief. He was sor - ry the seed that was shal -
let it fall down by the way. Or re - ceive it with glad - ness and wel -

dered a - loud   if the sown seed would live— or would die.   If the
low had died   but the good seed had grown— in be – lief,   But the
come the truth,   and be saved at the end— of the day!   And be

sown seed would live— or would die.   Grow lit - tle seeds,   'til the har-vest has come.
good seed had grown— in be – lief.
saved at the end— of the day!

Grow in the soil of my heart.   Grow lit - tle seeds,   'til the har - vest has come.

Keep on grow-ing. Keep on grow-ing, and I'll do my part.

3rd time to Coda

and I'll do my part.

2.The

Coda

JESUS GETS READY TO DIE

People in different countries eat their meals differently. When Jesus lived on earth in Palestine the food was placed on low tables. The men did not sit on low chairs but lay down on their sides on couches facing the food. Their feet were away from the table. As soon as the men were ready to eat, a servant or a child or sometimes a woman would walk around the tables, take off the men's sandals, and wash the dust off their feet. Today people don't do that but they sometimes take their visitors' coats and hang them in the closet for them. This makes the guests feel welcome. That's why in Jesus' day someone washed the visitors' feet.

One day Jesus and his disciples went to a house for supper, but something went wrong. Nobody took the guests' sandals and washed their dusty feet. This was most un-usual and rather rude. One of the younger disciples should have jumped up, gotten some water, and done the job, but nobody wanted to do it because that would make him look like a less important servant.

Instead, to everyone's surprise, Jesus got up off his couch, slowly took off his outer clothes, rolled up his sleeves, got a bowl of water, and walked to where Peter was lying on a couch waiting to have his feet washed so that he could start supper. Peter asked Jesus what he was doing, and Jesus said he was going to wash Peter's feet. Peter was very upset at that and said that he would never allow Jesus to do such a thing. Washing feet was work for a servant, not for the Lord Jesus.

Jesus told Peter if he wanted to re-main a disciple, he needed to have his feet washed by Jesus. Poor Peter was very confused but said he

wanted Jesus to wash all of him if that would mean he could still be a disciple. Jesus said that was not necessary and went ahead and washed Peter's feet. When Jesus finished he came back to his couch and explained what he had done. Jesus said that though the disciples did not understand what he had done, they would understand better in a few more days. He also said that they should then be like him and do the sorts of things he had done. The disciples were embarrassed and confused by the whole incident.

A few days later, a terrible thing happened. The Lord Jesus was taken by some wicked men and killed. They nailed him to a cross made of wood, and he died in great pain. But Jesus was not surprised that this happened to him. In fact, he had known it would happen and that was why he had washed the disciples' feet. He wanted them to remember that when he washed the dust off their feet with water and said that they must allow him to do it, he was preparing them for when he would wash away all his people's sin with his blood. After Jesus had died on the cross and came back from the dead the disciples understood why he had done such a humble thing as wash their feet. But they knew it was much more humble of him to die on the cross to wash away their sins. Jesus washes away the sins of anyone who believes that he is the Son of God.

Mark 15:39

Let's Pretend

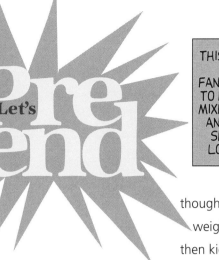

CHARLIE the COLT

WELL! I'M OFF TO SEE THE EXCITEMENT IN JERUSALEM. I'LL RIDE THIS APHID.

Charlie the colt stood with his mother quietly chewing hay. On the outside he looked very peaceful, but on the inside he was angry. Early that morning his master had come to him and said it was time he learned to carry a load.

Charlie had seen other little donkeys, including his mother, carrying great burdens. Sometimes he had seen little donkeys carrying such big men that the men's legs touched the ground on each side as they sat on the donkey. "They'll never get me loaded up like that!" Charlie had said to himself.

His master, a big man, had given Charlie a carrot. Charlie loved big, juicy carrots. Then the man had jumped on Charlie's back with a great thud. Charlie thought his back would break under the weight. He reared up on his front legs, then kicked his rear legs high in the air. His master gave a cry and fell to the ground with such a thwack that Charlie was sure he felt the earth quake.

Charlie's master was angry. He jumped up, grabbed a stick, and said, "I'll teach you a lesson, young Charlie! Who do you think you are? I feed you hay and carrots and when I need you to carry a load, you kick your hooves in the air. I'll teach you who's boss!" With that he hit Charlie and scolded him so Charlie would not do that again. When he got tired of scolding Charlie, the master went into his house limping and holding his back.

"Well," said Charlie's mother, a wise old donkey who was standing nearby while all this was happening, "now you know what it's like to be a donkey. Sometimes you get a carrot, other times you get a stick. You must learn that if you expect the master to feed you, he will expect you to work for him. If you work, you get carrots; if you don't, you get the stick. It's called the carrot-and-stick method."

Charlie now thought to himself, *I don't mind working, but why should that big man think he can jump on my back any time he wants to?*

Later that morning two men walked up to where Charlie and his mother were

67

standing. Charlie had never seen the men. Without a word they started to untie both donkeys and lead them away. Charlie wondered if the master was so angry with him that he had sold him to a stranger. *Can't be worse than the situation I'm in right now!* he thought.

Just then the master came running out of his house shouting, "Hey, what d'you think you are doing? Bring those donkeys back!"

The men stopped and, turning around, said, "The Master needs them."

Something very strange happened. When the men said, "The Master," Charlie's master looked as if he'd seen a ghost. "The Master? You mean the Messiah wants my donkeys? Then he must have them. Take them."

Charlie wondered who this "Master" was who could change his master so quickly.

The men led Charlie and his mother along the crowded, dusty streets. There were so many people that Charlie was glad the men held tightly to his halter, otherwise he might have gotten lost. "Don't worry, Charlie," said one of the men. "We'll look after you. We're taking you to the Master. He understands donkeys. He's kind and gentle and he wants you to do something special for him."

Charlie longed to be able to ask the men, "Who is the Master you speak about?" But they couldn't understand Donkeyese, and Charlie couldn't speak their language, although he understood some of it.

One of the men who seemed to be able to read Charlie's thoughts said, "The Master is God's Son, Charlie. He created all things, including donkeys. He gave you those big brown eyes and silky ears. He knows how heavy a load you can carry and will never give you more than you can manage. He understands donkeys."

Just then Charlie saw the Master. He was standing in the middle of a crowd of people, talking to them. There were old people and children and all of them were listening carefully to what he was saying. Charlie heard him say, "Come unto me, all you who are weary and heavy laden, and I will give you rest."

That's what I need, Charlie thought.

The Master turned, saw the men with the donkeys, and came over to Charlie. With the quietest voice Charlie had ever heard the Master said, "Now, Charlie, I know you don't like people sitting on you. But sometimes we have to do the things we are supposed to do even if we don't like them. But if we do them willingly we can grow to enjoy them." With that he patted Charlie on his muzzle and, laying a cloak across Charlie's shoulders, climbed gently on his back. "Let's go!" he said, and without so much as a snort, Charlie started walking.

The crowds started to cheer when they saw the Master. They threw branches in Charlie's way, but he didn't kick. They pushed and shoved him and got in his way, but the Master talked quietly to him, and Charlie kept walking in the direction the Master steered him. *I don't even know*

where I'm going, Charlie thought, *but it doesn't matter because the Master knows. He understands me, and I think he loves me too.*

Charlie had forgotten all about his mother who was trotting along beside him. He turned to her and said, "Momma, I'm sorry I kicked the master off my back. I might have hurt him badly."

She replied, "Well, Charlie, you shouldn't have done it, but he shouldn't have treated you the rough way he did. Look how differently this Master treats us."

Charlie laughed a donkey laugh (which doesn't sound like a laugh to humans) and said, "This is better than the carrot-and-stick method."

"I wish I could stay with the Master and work for him," Charlie said to his mother.

"I would like that too," Charlie's mother replied. "But I'm afraid it will not be possible."

It seemed as if the Master understood what Charlie and his mother were saying to each other in Donkeyese because he reached down and stroked Charlie's big, silky right ear. His touch was so gentle and firm. Then he leaned forward and whispered, "You're a good little donkey, Charlie. I'm pleased with you."

Charlie twisted his head around so that he could look into the Master's face. He was surprised to see the Master looking sad. There was a tear in his eye. Charlie wondered why he was sad when all the people were so pleased to see him. Charlie didn't know what the Master knew. Some of the rulers were already

planning to arrest Jesus. They wanted to have him killed.

I know what I'll do, Charlie thought to himself, *I'll cheer him up.* With that he started to trot, then he kicked his hind legs a little in the air. But not in the same way he had done to his owner. The Master held on tight and laughed, while Charlie's mother trotted as fast as she could to catch up. "Be careful, Charlie," she said. "Don't forget who is riding on your back."

"I won't, Mother," he replied, thinking to himself, *Why do mothers always have to say, "Be careful!"?*

Step 1

Thursday Evening 6—9 PM

Jesus and his disciples eat the Passover meal.

Step 2

Thursday night 9—midnight

Jesus in Garden of Gethsemane on Mount of Olives.

Jesus prays and disciples fall asleep.

Step 3

Friday morning just after midnight—3 AM

Judas comes to Gethsemane with band of armed guards.

Disciples run away.

Jesus is first taken to Annas, then to Caiaphas the high priest.

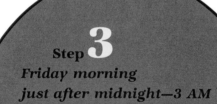

Step 4 *Early Friday morning 3—6 AM*

Sanhedrin come to Caiaphas' house for trial.

Outside in courtyard Peter denies that he knows Jesus.

Step 6 *Friday morning 9 AM—noon*
Roman soldiers scourge Jesus and lead him out to be crucified. Jesus is nailed to the cross.

Step 7 *Friday afternoon noon—3 PM*
Jesus dies.

Step 8 *Friday afternoon 3—6 PM*
Nicodemus and Joseph of Arimathea take Jesus' body and lay it in a new tomb.

Step 5 *Friday morning 6—9 AM*
Jesus is taken to Pilate. Pilate sends him to Herod. Herod sends him back to Pilate. Pilate condemns him. Roman soldiers scourge Jesus and lead him out to be crucified.

Step 9 *Sunday morning 6—9 AM*
Jesus' disciples find the tomb empty. Jesus is risen from the dead. He is alive forevermore.

JESUS & ME

Do you feel sorry for yourself and maybe cry when you have to do something you think is too hard or too scary? Maybe some medical things must be done to you that you think will be too painful. Talk to Jesus about your fear and hurts and pain. He knows all about that because he did some things that were hard and scary for him to do. Ask Jesus to be very close to you and help you. He will be there. Just ask him.

Fancy Footnotes

Let's Make a Video about Jesus

PARTICIPANTS ARE ENCOURAGED TO EXPAND AND **IMPROVISE**, USING THIS MATERIAL AS A GUIDE. ALLOW YOUR **IMAGINATION** TO "PEEK AROUND THE CORNER OF THE VERSE" AND SEE WHO IS COMING.

DO YOU HAVE TO USE BIG WORDS LIKE "IMPROVISE" AN' "IMAGINATION"?

Your Family Video Theater

The Centurion and His Wife

Cast: centurion, wife

Scene: A Roman officer (called a centurion because he is in charge of a hundred soldiers) arrives home and is greeted by his wife.

Wife	Greetings, husband. Welcome home. Did you have another busy day dealing with those troublesome Jews?
Centurion	*(quietly)* I had a busy day but not with "those troublesome Jews."
Wife	*(looking up quickly)* What d'you mean?
Centurion	I don't think I want to talk about it right now.
Wife	All right. Let's have dinner. I have asked the servant to cook some fresh fish from the Jordan River.
Centurion	*(pushing his food away)* I'm sorry, dear. I'm not hungry.
Wife	*(surprised)* Whatever is the matter? Are you ill?
Centurion	No, I'm not ill. Just worried.
Wife	Why? It's not like you to worry about anything.
Centurion	Well, I had to oversee a crucifixion today. . . .
Wife	*(interrupting)* Don't tell me a crucifixion is bothering you. As far as I can see, these rebellious Jews deserve it. Crucify them all, I say; then we can go back to Rome and leave this awful place and these awful people.
Centurion	It's not like that. I've been in charge of more crucifixions than I care to remember, but never one like this one.
Wife	*(interested now)* What was different about this one?
Centurion	It was the man called Jesus of Nazareth. . . .

Wife	(*interrupting again*) I've heard of him. A preacher, isn't he? Seems to get the religious people upset because he tells them things they don't want to hear. He was crucified?
Centurion	Yes, he was, and I was in charge because my junior officers were on leave.
Wife	Well, what was different about it?
Centurion	His attitude.
Wife	His attitude? How was that different?
Centurion	When the soldiers hammered the nails through his hands and feet he was in great pain, but he almost seemed to be assisting them. He didn't struggle. And I'm sure I heard him say something like, "Father, forgive them. They don't understand."
Wife	Was his father there?
Centurion	No. He calls God his Father. He said that he had come from the Father to do his will on earth and then he was going back to the Father.
Wife	Sounds weird to me.
Centurion	It's anything but weird, I can tell you.
Wife	Why do you say that?
Centurion	Because in the middle of the day the sun stopped shining, and there wasn't a cloud in the sky. It was eerie. It was as if the Father was saying, "This really is my Son, and I won't let you people laugh at and mock him in his pain."
Wife	If I didn't know you better I would think you had become one of his followers.
Centurion	Well, my dear wife, I don't know if I could be called one of his followers, but he made a believer out of me.
Wife	What d'you mean? You're a Roman. We have our gods. The Jews have theirs. What d'you mean he made a believer out of you?
Centurion	I mean that when I heard him on that cross say very quietly something like, "Father, into your hands I put my spirit," and then lift up his head and shout at the top of his voice, "It is finished," I knew I had never ever seen a man die like that.
Wife	You mean you actually believe that he was God's Son like he said?

Centurion	Yes, I do.
Wife	Then why would God let his Son die? It doesn't make sense.
Centurion	He didn't let him die. We didn't take his life from him. He gave it up.
Wife	But why would he do that?
Centurion	One of my men told me that he had heard this Jesus say that he had come to die for people's sins and that he would rise again from the dead.
Wife	Rise again from the dead? I never heard of such a thing!
Centurion	You may think this weird, but I would not be surprised if he did. After the way I saw him die I would think he could do anything.
Wife	Well, let me tell you this. I don't think for a minute that he will rise again. But if he does, I will believe too.
Narrator	Three days later Jesus did rise from the dead just as he had said. The centurion was overjoyed. His wife too became a believer, just as she had promised. They went back to Rome and told many people there about Jesus dying and rising again. That's one way the good news of Jesus began to spread all over the world.

JESUS IS ALIVE AND GOES BACK TO HEAVEN

It was very early in the morning, so early it was still dark. Mary Magdalene, Joanna, Mary the mother of James, Salome, and some other women took spices they had prepared and began walking toward the tomb where Joseph and his friends had taken Jesus' body. The women wanted to use spices to prepare Jesus' dead body for burial. They were all very sad. Some of them had seen the Lord Jesus die the cruel death of crucifixion, yet it was hard to believe he had died. Now they were hurrying so they could do one last thing for him.

"How will we move the huge stone we saw the men roll across the grave?" one of the women asked.

"We can't do it alone," another said.

"Maybe the soldier who was left to guard the tomb will help us," suggested a third woman.

The women arrived at the rocky hills and caves outside the city, the place that was used as a cemetery. They walked toward the cave where Joseph and Nicodemus had lovingly carried the body of Jesus. As they turned the corner in front of the cave, they wondered if the soldiers would chase them away. Suddenly all three of them gasped!

"Look . . . look . . ." said Joanna, "someone must have been here before us. The stone has been rolled away from the entrance!"

"But the soldiers are gone. Who could have done it?" asked Mary, the mother of James.

Suddenly two men in clothes that glowed like lightning stood beside the women. Immediately the frightened women bowed down with their faces to the ground because they knew the men were angels.

"Why do you look for the living among the dead?" the men asked them. "He is not here; he has risen! Remember how he told you, while he was still with you in Galilee: 'The Son of Man must be delivered into the hands of sinful men, be crucified and on the third day be raised again.'"

"Come," said one of the angels, "see where Jesus was laid."

The angels stopped speaking, and the women slowly raised their heads to look at them, but the angels had disappeared. Afraid and shaking, the women got up to take a look at the tomb and to see where Jesus had been. They had watched Joseph and his friends put the body of Jesus there, but now the grave was empty except for the grave clothes they had put on Jesus. He wasn't there!

"Now I remember that Jesus did tell us all this would happen to him. Then he said he would rise again on the third day! Do you remember that?" Joanna said excitedly.

"We should go right now and tell the disciples about this!" said Salome.

And so they ran as fast as they could back to the disciples to tell them about the empty tomb and the angels saying that Jesus was alive.

Before they got to the disciples, Jesus himself met the women. "Greetings," he said. The women fell down and hugged his feet. They saw the gaping holes the nails had made in Jesus' feet. Then they knew for sure that Jesus—the same Jesus they had seen being crucified—was alive and was standing there in front of them. They were so happy but also terribly afraid at the same time.

Then the risen Lord Jesus spoke to them. "Don't be afraid. Go and tell my brothers to go to Galilee. There they will see me."

The women got up quickly and shook the dust off their clothes. Their feet hardly touched the ground as they hurried back to the city to tell the disciples that angels and Jesus himself had talked to them that morning.

The men listened to the women but did not believe them. "That's nonsense," they said. "People don't rise from the dead."

"Maybe ordinary people don't," said Mary the mother of James, "but Jesus isn't an ordinary person. He is the Son of God, and we tell you that we have seen him and talked with him. Believe us when we say he is risen."

Peter got up and ran to the tomb to see for himself if there was any truth to the story the women were telling. John followed behind and caught up with Peter. When they got to the tomb, John looked inside without going in. But Peter went in and saw that the grave clothes were lying flat in the shape of Jesus' body. The cloths that had been wound around Jesus' face were folded. Then Peter knew it was all true! Jesus Christ, the Son of God, had risen from the dead. None of his disciples would ever be the same again.

Let's Pretend

ASCENSION

THIS STORY, TOLD HERE AS A FANTASY MARRIED TO FACT, IS TO BE MIXED WITH FAITH AND LAUGHTER, SHARED WITH LOVE AND JOY.

HMMM!

YOU SEE, DOC HE DOESN'T BLINK

HMMM!

HE DOESN'T BREATHE OR WIGGLE ANYTHING

HMMM!

HE SAYS THE SAME THING OVER AND OVER

HMMM! HMMM HMMMM!

"Hello, Cloud."

"Hello yourself, Mountain," said Little Cloud.

"Well, Little Cloud, what will you do today?" rumbled the mountain.

"I've been sent here to wait for our Lord Jesus."

Mountain was surprised. "Why, I'm expecting him too."

"Look!" said Little Cloud. "Here he comes with his disciples."

"It's been a long time since the Wondermaker made us, Little Cloud."

"A long time, Mountain."

"Little Cloud, do you remember at cre-ation when you sat on my head, the flowers danced in joy, the ants built their high hills, and the giraffes found out not one of them was painted with the same spots as another?"

"Yes, yes, I remember, Mountain, when the Wondermaker came to see all he had made, he said it all was so very, very good."

For a short time, neither Little Cloud or Mountain said anything. Both of them were thinking about the happy time they had had watching all the animals playing and enjoying the brand new world.

Little Cloud asked Mountain, "How long do you think it has been since Satan came to spoil it all?"

"Well, I'm not sure. I know it was a long time ago."

"Mountain, have you been here all that time?"

"All that time, Little Cloud. My sister mountains have had God's Glory Cloud around their slopes and have seen God's finger write rules for sinful men on two big stones. My brother, the one named Calvary, was split in two when our Lord died."

"Little Cloud looked thoughtful and said, "I was there when our Lord talked with Moses and Elijah on one of your rela-

tive's rocky peaks. It was wonderful! Peter and James and John were there. They were so scared when the Glory Cloud came and God's voice said, 'This is my Son, listen to him.'"

"Look, Little Cloud, Jesus is almost here. Why do you think he is coming?"

"I don't know, Mountain, but I see the disciples—there's Peter, James, and John—I remember them. He must have told them to meet him here."

"Somehow, Little Cloud, somehow I think he's going home today."

"Back to heaven, you mean?"

"Yes, back to his throne in heaven. What a day! And how proud I will be if he's going back to heaven from one of my slopes."

"Oh! Then I'm going to carry him softly in my arms right to the doors of heaven. What joy! Listen, Mountain, here come the angels."

JESUS & ME

Jesus is coming back! The angels told the disciples, and they told everyone else. Of course, Jesus had also talked about his return before he died. How exciting! When will he come? Maybe today, or tomorrow, or before Christmas, or on another special day, such as Easter.

Jesus doesn't want Christians, even young Christians, to only look up to heaven and wait. He wants Christians to be busy doing his work until he comes. Doing his work means living for him, getting to know him better by reading his Word, and learning to pray. It means going to Sunday school, helping and caring for people, and telling friends and neighbors about the cross and how much Jesus loves them. Another thing Christians should be doing is telling people about Jesus' second coming. Many people don't know about that. They need to get ready for that too.

Angels are called morning stars, wind, fire, God's messengers, but never sons or daughters of God.

Sometimes angels look like people; sometimes they are bright and shiny.

Angels have no wings.
Angels do not marry.
Angels constantly praise God.
Angels are very powerful.

Angels protect and help God's people.

Three angels are named in the Bible: Michael, Gabriel, Satan.

Angels sang at the birth of Jesus; they will be with him when he comes again.

Angels are not bothered by light or darkness. They can see in the dark and in Revelation 19:17 John tells about an angel who stood in the sun without being uncomfortable.

Angels deliver special messages to God's people, sometimes in a dream and sometimes by coming to talk with them.

Angels are older than the earth and they do not die. (They are immortal.)

THEY USED ABOUT 120 POUNDS OF SPICES.

JESUS' BODY WAS WRAPPED IN STRIPS OF CLOTH LIKE THIS. THE STRIPS WERE PAINTED WITH GOOEY SPICES AND WRAPPED AROUND HIS BODY BEFORE BURIAL.

Fancy Footnotes

Let's Make a Video about Jesus

HMMMMMMMMM
HMM HMMMMMMMMM
HM HMMMM
HMM HMMMMMM,
HMMM HMM HMMMM
HM H HMMM.
HMMMM HMMM
HMMMMMMM HM
"HMMM HMMMM
HMM HMMMM
HM HMM HMMMM"
HMM HMM HMM HM
"HMMMMM
HM HMM HMMM."

HE'S CURED!
HE'S CURED!
THANKS DOC!
HOW MUCH DO I
OWE YA?

Your Family Video Theater

Seeing
Is
Believing

HMMM!

Cast: The eleven disciples, Jesus, two servant girls—Lois and Joanna

Scene: Two rooms—servant quarters and upper room

Narrator	After Jesus suffered and died he rose again. He appeared to his disciples over a period of forty days and gave many convincing proofs that he was alive.

Servant girls are preparing a meal.

Lois	Joanna, do you believe the story that's been going around, that Jesus has come back from the dead?
Joanna	I don't know what to think. I didn't believe it until a week ago. I was on duty here at old Ebenezer's house. He had lent his big room to the disciples who were hiding out after the crucifixion. I had taken the food up to them and heard them bolt the door after me. I tell you, Lois, that door is as thick as my fist, and the bolts are made of iron.
Lois	I know. What happened?
Joanna	Well, when I took the food to the men, there wasn't a sound. Those who were talking were whispering. They looked scared out of their wits.

PETER LOOKED IN THE CAVE ON EASTER MORNING. HE SAW THAT THE STRIPS OF CLOTH WERE STILL WRAPPED IN PLACE BUT JESUS WAS GONE.

THIS BUG WILL NEVER GET OUT OF HIS WRAPPINGS

JESUS LEFT THE TOMB EVEN BEFORE THE ANGELS ROLLED THE STONE DOOR AWAY.

HEY, MOVE THAT STONE! I'M COMIN' OUT!

Lois	No wonder! If the Romans crucified Jesus, their leader, what would they do to his followers? And his followers were in that room.
Joanna	After I came downstairs I heard loud noises. There were some happy shouts and some singing behind that locked door. I ran up the stairs and listened, and I tell you, Lois, I heard the voice of Jesus in there.
Lois	How did you know it was his voice?
Joanna	I would know it anywhere. I used to go and listen to him preach.
Lois	How did Jesus get in?
Joanna	That's it—I don't know. The door was still bolted. I tried the handle. What's more, no one could have gotten past me without my seeing them. The kitchen is at the bottom of the stairs and besides, the outside door was also locked because the disciples were afraid of the Jewish leaders.
Lois	What happened next?
Joanna	Well, the disciples came pounding down the stairs talking loudly about Jesus just appearing—as if he'd come right through the walls—and disappearing the same way. They told me the whole thing.
Lois	Was it his ghost? Ghosts can go through locked doors and walls—
Joanna	No, it was Jesus, really his real body. I asked Peter if it was a ghost, and he said, "No, Joanna, I wondered that myself. But Jesus saw our doubts and asked us for a piece of fish and ate it right in front of us." Just think, Lois, they said Jesus ate a piece of fish I cooked!
Lois	Ghosts don't eat fish. It must have been Jesus.
Joanna	I know, I know, but I still don't know—
Lois	I believe it, Joanna. Jesus straightened my brother's withered hand. I saw it happen with my own eyes.

Disciples arrive talking, greet the girls cheerfully.

Thomas	Shalom, Joanna and Lois. I hear you had some excitement last week when I wasn't here.
Lois	Shalom, sir. Joanna tells me Jesus came to dinner, right through the wall. Joanna finds it difficult to believe, but I believe it happened, even though I wasn't there either.

Matthew *(to Thomas)*	Thomas, you are such a doubter. All of us saw him, talked to him.
Thomas	Unless I see the nail marks in his hands, touch them, and put my hand into the gaping wound the soldiers made in his side with their spear, I will not believe it.

Disciples go into room, bolt door; servant girls busy themselves with preparations. Suddenly there is a commotion as before. Girls run to the door, try it, find it locked, and press ears "mime" fashion to it, listening. Action is on other side: Jesus has entered and calls Thomas forward.

Jesus	Shalom, Thomas! Put your finger here *(offers hands)*. See my hands. Reach out your hand and put it into my side. Stop doubting and believe.

The servant girls clutch each other and jump up and down with joy.

Joanna	I believe! Oh! I believe! Even though I cannot see him through this door, I believe!
Thomas	*(to Jesus as he drops at Jesus' feet)* My Lord and my God!
Jesus	Because you have seen me, Thomas, you have believed. Blessed are those who have not seen and yet have believed.
Lois	He's talking about us, Joanna. We haven't seen him, but we believe. Yes, we believe. He blesses us for our faith! We must tell our friends and our families that Jesus is truly alive.

Freeze all characters.

Narrator	There are so many other things Jesus did while the disciples watched. They are not recorded in the Bible. But the miracles that are written down in the Bible are recorded there so that all of us who are like Lois and Joanna, who have not seen Jesus with our own eyes will believe that Jesus is the Christ, the Son of God. When we believe that, we will have eternal life.

WHAT IS IT?

I THINK IT'S JUST A WARM, HAPPY, FRIENDLY SHAPE.

While he was blessing them, he left them and was taken up into heaven. Luke 24:51

Springtime

Words and Music by
STUART BRISCOE and LARRY MOORE

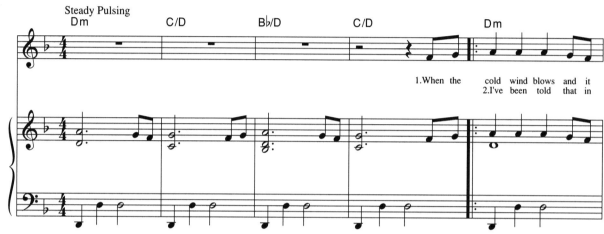

1.When the cold wind blows and it
2.I've been told that in

free-zes my nose and it sleets and snows then the e-very-one knows we're all read-y, Je-sus,
days of old when the night was cold and the stone was rolled,

Am7 ... **Dm** ... **Gm7** ... **Am7**

read - y for the spring.
Je - sus rose a - gain.

we're all read - y,
Je - sus,

read - y for the
Je - sus rose a -

Dm ... **C/D** ... **B♭/D**

spring.
gain.

When the night is bleak and the raft - ers creak and the floor-boards squeak
There is more, my friend, that's not the end, the sky will rend and

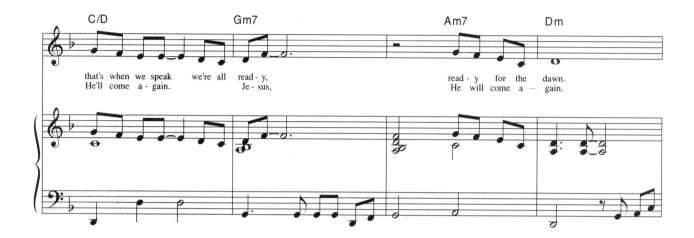

that's when we speak we're all read-y, read-y for the dawn.
He'll come a-gain. Je-sus, He will come a — gain.

we're all read-y, read-y for the dawn.
Je-sus, He will come a-gain.

Spring-time, spring-time, ring-a-ling-a-ding-time, spring-time, spring-time we're read-y for spring.
Spring-time, spring-time, ring-a-ling-a-ding-time, spring-time, spring-time, Je-sus rose a-gain.

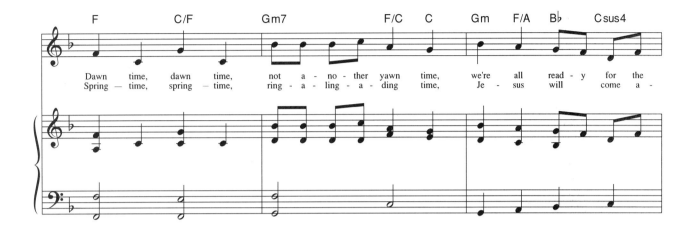

Dawn time, dawn time, not a - no - ther yawn time, we're all read - y for the
Spring — time, spring — time, ring - a - ling - a - ding time, Je - sus will come a -

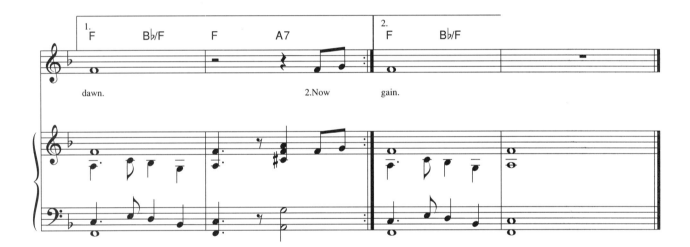

dawn.   2.Now   gain.

When Jesus was crucified, his disciples were very frightened. They thought that they might be killed too. But something wonderful happened. Jesus rose from the dead and met with the disciples. They were amazed at first, but then they became very excited. Jesus truly was the Son of God! He had said so all along, but now they were sure. He had defeated death and was alive forevermore.

Jesus said that he was going to heaven. He also said he would come back one day. He told the disciples they should make sure that everybody in the whole world knew that he had died for their sins and was alive again. The disciples wondered how they could possibly let everybody know. Jesus said he would send the Holy Spirit who would be with them and would help them to be brave and do what Jesus wanted them to do. Then Jesus left the disciples. They watched him go up in the air until a cloud covered him and they could no longer see him.

Soon Jesus kept his promise. He sent the Holy Spirit, and right away the disciples were very brave. They could even preach sermons and talk to rulers without being afraid. They began to tell everybody about Jesus. Many people believed and became Christians. On Pentecost, the day Jesus sent the Holy Spirit, Peter, who had been one of the most frightened disciples when Jesus was killed, stood up and told the people of Jerusalem that Jesus was alive. That day three thousand people became Christians.

THE ACTS OF THE APOS

Not everyone believed Peter. Some rulers were jealous because so many people were leaving the synagogues. Others became angry and were willing to do almost anything to get the people to stop talking about Jesus.

But God took care of the new Christians. One of the men who wanted to kill every Christian he could find was named Saul. God knew just how to make Saul into a Christian. And he did. Suddenly Saul, the man who wanted to kill Christians, was working as hard as he could to tell as many people as he could find that Jesus was the Son of God.

The Book of Acts was written by a doctor, Luke, who also wrote the Gospel of Luke. No, Luke wasn't one of the twelve apostles, but probably Luke had spent a lot of time watching Jesus and listening to him. The important thing was that Luke believed Jesus was the Son of God and wanted to tell his friend Theophilus, who was probably a ruler, all about what Jesus had done and taught. Luke also wanted his friend to know how the early Christians went out to tell people about Jesus. So Luke wrote about Peter and Paul and other leaders of the early church. All of them were busy, busy people.

There are other stories from the Book of Acts in *Paul Hits the Beach: And Other Wild Adventures,* Book 4 of the series, Baker Interactive Books for Lively Education.

LUKE

Luke was not one of the twelve disciples but he spent a lot of time with Jesus and in the Gospel of Luke he kept writing and writing about all the things Jesus did while he was on earth. Many exciting things also happened after Jesus went back to heaven. So Luke continued writing the rest of the story in the Book of Acts. This is one of the first amazing events he wrote about in his second book.

Just before Jesus ascended into heaven, he told his disciples to wait in Jerusalem until the Holy Spirit came. The Holy Spirit is the third person of the Trinity. Jesus promised that the Holy Spirit would give his people power to do his work. As they waited Peter talked to everyone who had gathered in the upper room. They needed to replace Judas Iscariot who had betrayed Jesus. Peter said the man needed to be someone who had

been with Jesus like the other disciples had—right from the day Jesus started his ministry.

The names of two good followers of Jesus were suggested. The whole group prayed, asking God to show them which one of the two God had chosen to be the twelfth disciple in place of Judas. God showed them it should be Matthias. From then on Matthias was called one of the twelve apostles.

Forty days after Jesus ascended there was a special feast day, the day of Pentecost. The apostles were hoping this would be the day for the Holy Spirit to come. They were busy waiting and becoming more and more excited. More than 120 followers of Jesus gathered in the upper room on Pentecost, waiting just as Jesus had told them to.

Suddenly all sorts of strange and wonderful things began to happen. First there was a sound. It was a

noise like an incredible wind. The Bible doesn't say it was a wind—just that it sounded like a wind. It was so loud though that everyone in the city heard it and came running to the room where the followers of Jesus were waiting. That was where the noise was coming from.

Meanwhile, inside the room other unusual things were happening. As the apostles looked at each other they saw what seemed to be tongues of fire—not real tongues of fire, though it looked like that—sitting on everyone's head. This was how the Holy Spirit came at Pentecost.

The disciples burst out into the street to tell everyone what had happened. The Holy Spirit had been given just as the prophets had promised. People in the crowd that had gathered were from every part of the country and from outside the country. There were foreigners in Jerusalem to celebrate the feast of Pentecost. All of them heard in their own language the good news about Jesus! They were amazed but not as amazed as the apostles who heard themselves speaking in languages that they had never learned. What a miracle!

Peter got up and explained to everyone what was happening. God the Father had sent his Spirit as God the Son had promised. The Spirit would live inside the followers. The Spirit made people listen to Peter so that many of them became believers that day and they all joined the church. This was the birthday of the Church of Jesus Christ

Luke wrote down all these things in a letter he sent to a Greek man named Theophilus. Luke wanted his friend to know exactly what happened on that exciting day in Jerusalem. He wanted us to know too. Read about it in Acts, chapters one and two.

bringing We are to to the living news, you telling turn . . . good you living God. Acts 14:15

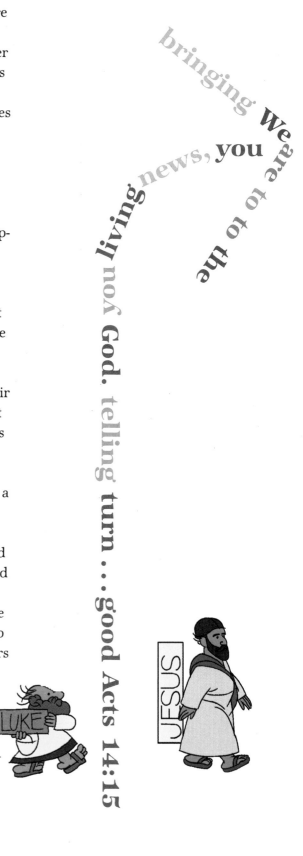

Let's Pretend

A LOOK AT LUKE

Marcus and Lucas were great friends. Sometimes they argued and fought, but that's how some boys show they are friends. They lived in a lovely city full of shady trees that grew on the bank of a fast-flowing river. Marcus was six months older than Lucas. He could always run just a little faster, and when they wrestled he usually won. But Lucas was a better student. He got higher grades than Marcus.

One bright spring day the boys asked permission to go fishing. Their mothers were nervous about their going to the river alone. "We'll bring back fish for supper if you'll only let us go!" they pleaded.

"All right," their mothers had replied, "but don't go falling into the water. Don't do anything silly."

"No, Mother," they had both said to their mothers in the same way that boys all over the world speak when they think their mothers worry too much.

"Now, remember," Marcus's mother had called after them as they ran down the path carrying their nets and lunches, "don't fall in the water. And if you go and drown yourselves, don't come running to me for sympathy." The boys laughed. They knew that Marcus's mother worried about them, but she always had a little joke.

The snow was melting high in the mountains, filling the river with clear, cold, green water that roared and splashed as it flowed through the town. Marcus threw in his net and immediately he felt a great tug. "Help," he shouted to Lucas, "I think I've caught a whale!" It was not a whale but it was such a big fish that it pulled Marcus right off his feet. The fish, knowing it was caught in a net, swam as hard as it could up the river, pulling the net with Marcus hanging on as he was dragged across the grassy bank. "Help!" he cried again. Lucas ran as fast as he could to catch up with his friend who was being dragged headfirst closer and closer to the rushing river.

Lucas dived at Marcus's legs, grabbed them with one arm, and tried to hold on to a tree with the other arm. But the fish

99

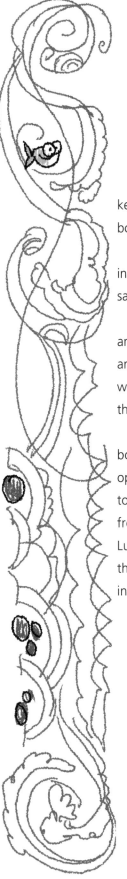

kept swimming and now it was pulling both Marcus and Lucas.

"Let go of the net or you'll be pulled into the river," said an old woman who saw their predicament.

But Marcus would not let go of the net, and Lucas would not let go of his friend, and the fish did not want to be caught. So with a big splash Marcus and Lucas joined the fish in the rushing river.

The river was flowing so fast that the boys were swept up in its current in the opposite direction to the fish. The net was torn from Marcus's hand, so the fish got free and took Marcus's net with him. But Lucas held on to his friend, and together they were swept along in the cold, rushing water.

Suddenly the boys felt themselves pulled sideways toward the bank. Another fisherman had seen their dangerous situation and quickly threw his net in their path. And he had caught them! But the force of the water and the weight of the boys was almost too much for him. He called for help, and soon a number of men hauled the boys safely to the bank. They lay there gasping for breath, shivering in their wet clothes.

"Quick," said Andrew, the man who had caught them in his net, "we must get these boys into some dry clothes." With that the men carried the boys to the home across the street. Soon they were wrapped in warm blankets, sipping hot drinks, and feeling a lot better.

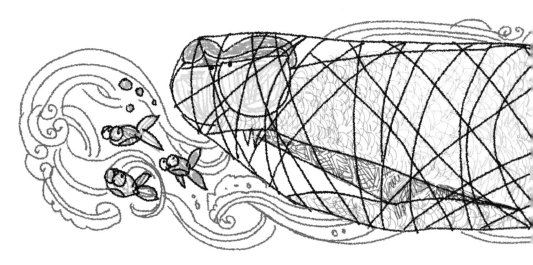

"What are we going to tell our mothers?" the boys wondered.

"Tell them the truth," Andrew replied. "Always tell the truth."

"They'll never believe the truth," Marcus responded with a grin.

Andrew and his neighbor Theophilus were looking at Lucas's notebook, which, along with his clothes, was drying by the fire.

"This is very interesting, Lucas. You seem to make notes about everything. What do you want to be when you grow up? A reporter?"

"No, I want to be a doctor. Marcus wants to be a soldier. I don't. I'd rather heal people than hurt them."

"Well, that's because you're not brave enough to be a soldier!" Marcus shouted, getting red in the face.

"Now, boys," said Salome, Andrew's wife, who had three sons and understood boys, "this is no time for arguments. Don't forget, doctors sometimes need soldiers to protect them, and soldiers need doctors to dress their wounds."

"Who knows," said Andrew "perhaps the Lord will allow you to be a doctor and a reporter."

"What do you mean—the Lord?" asked Marcus. "Is that the same as the gods?"

"No," Andrew said, "we believe there is one God who will send his son Jesus into the world to be our Savior."

"Savior? What's a savior?" asked Marcus.

Lucas chuckled and said, "Someone who pulls two boys out of a rushing river!"

"That's right," Andrew replied, "but God's Son will save us from much more than rushing rivers."

By this time the boys' clothes were dry so they dressed quickly and got ready to leave. "Thank you so much, Mr. Andrew and Mrs. Salome," they said. "You have been so very kind to us."

"By the way," Lucas said to the neighbor as he was leaving the house, "May I ask you a question?"

"Certainly," the neighbor replied.

"Your name—Theophilus—means lover of God, doesn't it?"

"You're absolutely right, Lucas. Some of my friends are lovers of God because they say he has first loved us," Theophilus said. "But I'm not so sure about him and his teachings. My friends are trying to tell me that Jesus is the promised Messiah. But I'm not convinced yet. Maybe someday . . ."

"I'd like to hear more about God loving us," Lucas said, "but it's getting dark and our mothers will be worrying about us. May I come some other time to hear about a God who loves us?"

Andrew and Salome smiled a very happy smile and said, "Certainly, if your parents agree."

So both Marcus and Lucas visited Andrew and Salome many times. Sometimes neighbor Theophilus would come over and listen. As the boys learned about God's love for them, they learned to love the Lord too.

After many visits, Andrew asked Lucas, "Do you still want to be a doctor who takes notes?"

Lucas said immediately, "I certainly do! That would be wonderful!"

Andrew gave Lucas a happy hug and said, "You know, Lucas, I have a strong feeling that one day you will be a doctor who travels the world taking notes so that you can write about the love of God."

Neighbor Theophilus was smiling too.

"Who knows," said Luke, "maybe I'll send you a letter, Mr. Theophilus. Maybe I can tell you things that will help you believe in a God who loves you."

•

Years later when Lucas became Dr. Luke, he traveled with the apostle Paul all over the world. Wherever Luke went he took careful notes and then he wrote two wonderful books about God's son, the Lord Jesus, who lived on earth while Luke was a doctor. Those books are in the Bible—The Gospel of Luke and The Acts of the Apostles. Guess the name of the man who received the first copy of Luke's books.

LUKE & ME

Do you think Luke always liked writing? Maybe he worked really hard in school learning to do that. You may like writing or math or art. Maybe Luke played "doctor" when he was young and pretended to write prescriptions. Anyway, when he grew up, he became a real doctor and traveled with Paul helping him to tell people about Jesus.

Luke kept a diary and wrote down everything that happened. He was as careful in writing his books, Luke and Acts, as he was about treating his patients. He knew it was very important to get everything right.

You need to work hard in school too, especially at the things you do easily and well. We never know how God will want to use you for his work when you grow up.

Luke couldn't use a pen or pencil or typewriter or computer for his letters. He used parchments made of sheep skins or goat skins, or maybe the skin of another animal.

Scrolls were rolled up around a wooden rod or folded carefully and sealed with a wax seal that had to be broken before the scrolls could be read.

Paul's letter to the Romans would have needed a scroll about thirteen feet long. Some groups of people, such as Essenes, preserved scrolls in pottery jars and put the jars in caves, where they were found hundreds of years later.

In the synagogue schools, teachers used wax-covered wooden tablets and a stylus (a small piece of wood sharpened on one end) to make letters. The wax could be scraped off and the tablet used again.

Pieces of broken pottery scratched with a sharp point were used as scrap paper.

Ink was made from the diluted gum of a myrrh tree or powdered charcoal. Ink wells were made of pottery. Pens were made from reeds that were split and sharpened at one end to form a point.

Let's Make a Video about

PARTICIPANTS ARE ENCOURAGED TO EXPAND AND IMPROVISE, USING THIS MATERIAL AS A GUIDE. ALLOW YOUR IMAGINATION TO "PEEK AROUND THE CORNER OF THE VERSE" AND SEE WHO IS COMING.

Luke

Your Family Video Theater

John Mark

Cast: Aris, Archi, John Mark

Scene: Room with three chairs and other simple furniture.

Narrator	Luke wrote the story about John Mark, a young believer, who had been invited by his Uncle Barnabas to travel with him and the famous apostle Paul on a missionary journey. John Mark was excited to be asked, and off he went. But to everybody's surprise he returned home without the other men. His friends wondered why.
Aris	Welcome home, John Mark. Glad to see you!
Archi	That's right. We were worried about you. We prayed for you.
John Mark	Thanks, guys. Glad to be back. Glad to see you. Thanks for your prayers.
Aris	Well, tell us about the trip. Was it a lot of fun?
John Mark	No, it wasn't a lot of fun. Not at all!
Archi	Sounds like a bummer. Did you have a hard time?
John Mark	Yes, I sure did. I don't know what I expected when I set off with Uncle Barnabas and Paul, but I had some surprises.
Aris	Like what? What happened?
Archi	Yeah, what? You went to preach the gospel, didn't you? Weren't the people glad to see you? Didn't they thank you for coming?
John Mark	No, they weren't all glad to see us. The first place we went to we met a man called Elymas (EEL-AH-MAAHS). He was weird. Paul said Elymas was full of evil and was trying to stop the

106

gospel from being preached. Then Paul said Elymas would become blind as a punishment for being so evil.

Aris	Wow! What happened? Did he become blind?
John Mark	He sure did!
Archi	That's scary. What did you do?
John Mark	What did I do? I tried to look like I wasn't there.
Aris	What happened then?
John Mark	Well, that's the bad news. The good news is that a very important man named Sergius Paulus (SIR-JAS PAW-LAAHS) became a Christian. That was exciting.
Archi	Did you go anywhere else?
John Mark	Yes, we sailed from the country of Cyprus to a place called Perga in Pamphylia (PAAM-FIL-EE-AH).
Aris	Perga in what?
John Mark	Pamphylia. Didn't you learn geography in school?
Aris	Of course, I did. I wanted to make sure you knew where it was!
John Mark	C'mon. Admit it. You always had trouble with geography. Math was your favorite subject.
Archi	Sounds like a nice place.
John Mark	It wasn't nice. Hot and sticky. Lots of sickness. In fact, Paul got very sick there and wanted to leave for another place where it was cooler and he could get well again. But it was a very difficult and dangerous journey to that town.
Aris	So that's where you went next?
John Mark	Well, not exactly.
Archi	Not exactly? What does that mean? Did you go there, or not?
John Mark	Well, Uncle Barnabas and Paul went there, but I decided to come home.
Aris	You mean you came home on your own?
John Mark	Yes.
Archi	Why? Why did you leave?
John Mark	I don't want to talk about it.

John Mark gets up and leaves the room.

WOOP-EEEE!

THE END OF THE BOOK IS COMING!

Aris	That's strange, isn't it?
Archi	Why doesn't he want to talk about it? D'you think he got scared when he saw that Elymas fellow become blind?
Aris	Maybe. Or maybe he was homesick. After all, his mother does have one of the nicest homes in Jerusalem.
Archi	Maybe he felt left out because his Uncle Barnabas and Paul are older and are such close friends. Or maybe John Mark was afraid he would get sick like Paul did.
Aris	He didn't want to have anything to do with going on to that next place, did he?
Archi	I wonder what Paul thinks about this. After all, John Mark was supposed to be their helper.
Aris	Hmmm. Paul might be angry. Paul's a pretty tough guy, you know!
Archi	Right. But Uncle Barnabas is a gentle soul. I'd guess that he'd stick up for John Mark.
Aris	I suppose so. But let's not spend a lot of time guessing about this. Our friend is hurting and we've got to find ways to help him get over this.
Narrator	Years later the friends met Dr. Luke and told him this story. Luke included it in The Acts of the Apostles. John Mark later did work again with Uncle Barnabas. Yes, Paul was unhappy with John Mark but John Mark later became a great leader in the early church. Paul and John Mark became friends again and worked together for the Lord. John Mark wrote the Gospel of Mark.

PARTICIPANTS ARE ENCOURAGED TO EXPAND AND IMPROVISE, USING THIS MATERIAL AS A GUIDE. ALLOW YOUR IMAGINATION TO "PEEK AROUND THE CORNER OF THE. . . .

LET'S GO! YOU CAN KEEP SAYING IT IN THE NEXT BOOK!

These innovative books will appeal to parents who want to teach biblical truths to their children in a fresh and exciting way. The interactive presentation of Bible stories, using songs, drama, and cartoons, makes the **B.I.B.L.E.** books ideal for family devotions. Kids will actually look forward to spending time together learning about God's word. No more coaxing and cajoling.

This multi-media approach can add excitement and enrichment to other educational settings:

- Home school
- Christian school
- Children's church
- Sunday school

Songs and readings from these books are also available on audio.

Six adventures are waiting in each book of the **B.I.B.L.E.** series. Take an excursion with your family from creation through the New Testament. Look below at characters and events found in all four books:

$14.99 each • Hardback • 112 pages

Available now:

Moses Takes a Road Trip
And Other Famous Journeys

- *Creation*
- *Adam and Eve*
- *Noah*
- *Abram*
- *Moses*
- *Joshua*

ISBN 0-8010-4183-X

Jesus Makes a Major Comeback
And Other Amazing Feats

- *John the Baptist*
- *Jesus' Birth*
- *Jesus' Miracles*
- *Jesus' Big Week*
- *Jesus' Resurrection*
- *Luke*

ISBN 0-8010-4197-X

Coming in 1997:

David Drops a Giant Problem
And Other Fearless Heroes

- *Samuel*
- *David*
- *Solomon*
- *Jeremiah*
- *Daniel*
- *Jonah*

ISBN 0-8010-4216-X

Paul Hits the Beach
And Other Wild Adventures

- *Peter*
- *Paul's Life*
- *Paul's Journeys*
- *Timothy*
- *James*
- *John*

ISBN 0-8010-4202-X

Jill and **Stuart Briscoe** are the parents of three grown children and the grandparents of nine. Jill has written more than forty books, and Stuart more than fifty. Stuart serves as senior pastor of Elmbrook Church in Brookfield, Wisconsin. Jill is an advisor to women's ministries at the church, and director of Telling the Truth media and ministries. Both are worldwide speakers at retreats and conferences. The Briscoes live in Oconomowoc, Wisconsin.

Russ Flint is the designer/illustrator of many children's books, including *Let's Make a Memory, Let's Hide a Word, My Very First Bible,* and *Teach Me About Jesus.* He regularly contributes artwork to such magazines as *Ideals* and *Guideposts for Kids* and is cofounder of Dayspring Card Company. He has also illustrated such familiar classics as *Legend of Sleepy Hollow, A Christmas Carol, Swan Lake,* and *Little Women.* He lives in Greenville, California.

Why is it important to believe Jesus is alive?

Why doesn't an angel talk to me?

How can I show that I am sorry for doing Bad things?